Crusty Crones Get Out and About

The cauldron has been stirred,
where next?

Crusty Crones
Get Out
and About

The cauldron has been stirred,
where next?

Kimi Ravensky

and

Harmonia Saille

BOOKS

Winchester, UK
Washington, USA

First published by O-Books, 2011
O Books is an imprint of John Hunt Publishing Ltd., The Bothy, Deershot Lodge, Park Lane, Ropley,
Hants, SO24 0BE, UK
office1@o-books.net
www.o-books.com

For distributor details and how to order please visit the 'Ordering' section on our website.

A CIP catalogue record for this book is available from the British Library.

Design: Stuart Davies

Cover Image and Black & White Illustrations by Kimi Ravensky

Printed in the UK by CPI Antony Rowe
Printed in the USA by Offset Paperback Mfrs, Inc

We operate a distinctive and ethical publishing philosophy in all
areas of our business, from our global network of authors to
production and worldwide distribution.

CONTENTS

4 Moots, Groups, Covens and Gatherings

5 Broom Closet and Other Issues

6 Rites of Passage with Kimi

Appendices

Acknowledgements

Kimi Ravensky would like to thank:
Harmonia who went above and beyond the call of any author/editor, and sorted and made some semblance of sense of my ravings and ramblings.

Pog the black cat with two white whiskers who is responsible for changing my life, and Binky and Mutley for being at my feet when it was cold.

Teague the best son anyone could ever have.

Pearly, Rowan and Jonno, who helped with the technology computer stuff.

Shannon for being at the end of my first alone journey in Oz

Matthew for looking out for me.

Shourie as we have travelled together on many different levels

Isaac Bonewits (may he rest in peace in the Summerlands), Cassandra Eason, Janet Farrar and Gavin Bone for inspired thoughts and training and it's a pity I didn't listen because I had my bum kicked, but will do so in future.

The Australian pagan community for providing some fabulous adventures/mischief and a bit of pixie mayhem.

The universe for all the wonders adventures discoveries and crap I have been through.

Harmonia Saille would like to thank:
Kimi of course for making me laugh and being patient through all my whining in my vertigo attack months.

Husband Rick for his patience and technical expertise, and children Mikey Dunne and Sarina van Ruth for their input.

Again Janet and Gavin along with Del and Bev Richardson, and Anna Franklin for showing me some great rituals and who are forever wise.

All at the Limerick and Clare Pagan Moots, especially Daithi O Laoidhigh and Bernie and Simon.

Ray Sweeney of the Pagan Federation Ireland.

Hedge and all at White Wicca.

Morgana Sythove of Pagan Federation International.

All at Witchdom, especially my good friends Lady Orchid, Vita Remue, Arnametia, Aradia and Marti.

Preface

In becoming a pagan you will have surely had a calling and embarked on lots of study and practice, even if you are still seeking your own personal path. Born with homing pigeon blood in your heart, you read a book, then more books, you heard a story from Aunty Ethel, or made a conscious or unconscious choice. You may have read Jungian theory and it made you wonder, or you may have discovered something that you like and that fits you, and bought books on the weird and wonderful, from angels to tarot and witches to druids, New Age, "Old Age," crystals, meditation and magic. These books are usually in a back corner of the book store, and you regularly skulked in that corner until the paranoia set in when someone glanced in your general direction, so you grabbed a book that looked interesting and left as quickly as possible.

This paranoia passed though, and over a short period of time you owned that corner. Have you already noticed that you read bits of books that suited you over and over again? What happened was discovery!

If this is describing you, where do you go now? You have some knowledge, but what do you do with it? Who can you share your thoughts with? Perhaps now is the time to get out and about into the wonderful world of pagans. The adventure begins.

Bright Blessings

Kimi Ravensky and **Harmonia Saille**

Kimi Ravensky meets Harmonia Saille

Kimi Ravensky came to write this book because of an event involving her black cat, Pog, and a chance friendship with Harmonia. The event ended her career as she knew it.

Owing to one thing or another she is here and you are reading her words. She was out of action for several months, but discovered the power that has been lying dormant for a long time. She couldn't walk, so fell back into arts and crafts and discovered the computer. Another door opened which was an unexpected and complete surprise...she seemed to be able to write, and has now had several articles published in a Southern Hemisphere magazine, an Australia-wide magazine and has her own column with an e-zine.

In this book, Kimi will tell you all about life out there in the pagan world, what to expect at gatherings and about pagans in general, from what they wear and how they may act to what pathway they may follow.

For **Harmonia Saille**, spirituality has always been foremost in her life and her background of Irish, Manx and Welsh, and a family ability to see strange phenomena has had some influence on this. Having astral travelled since a small child, Harmonia drifted in to hedgewitchery, as a natural progression of her interests in contact with spirit, otherworldly travelling, nature, herbal lore, divination, folklore and magic. Harmonia's articles have appeared in various spiritual magazines internationally and she is co-editor of Irish Pagan Magazine, Brigid's Fire. She holds workshops locally in Ireland where she lives and at international events.

It was a number of deliberating illnesses which led to Harmonia writing her first book *The Spiritual Runes* and her maladies eventually under control, she wrote a second *Walking the Faery Pathway*. Harmonia met Kimi by chance on a popular pagan forum and loved her lively, fresh, and humorous approach to life and this book became a joint affair.

Harmonia gets out and about in events, nature and the Otherworld.

Kimi Ravensky's *Down to Earth Guide* on Pagans, Rituals, Large Gatherings, and Fashion

Gatherings

As a witch or pagan who has been following a pathway for a couple of years, at this point you should be reasonably aware of the seasonal celebrations and that most likely there will be a gathering or festival somewhere close to a large city, or perhaps in a more rural location. You might know by now the bookstores and other pagan friendly places or sites on the internet. It's a matter of asking what's going on and when, where and how much, so stick your nose in every place you can think of. Another thing that seems to happen is that the information is drawn to you, it's as if you are doing a subconscious spell — you are attracting the information to come to you. So look out for it.

In countries in both the Southern and Northern Hemisphere and most certainly in Australia and the UK, there are regular gatherings and festivals throughout the year on or around the sabbats or solstices and equinoxes. The most important thing to do is to plan for them. Most people can only attend one or two a year for reasons of finances, family, or time off work, school, or university. It's an idea to pick one that you relate to. Yule for example is family friendly, where Beltaine is often for those over eighteen years.

Let's just say a gathering is coming up, you want to go but can't afford it, didn't plan, and just found it on a random site, in a magazine or on a flyer. If so, then it's time for the hunter-gathering for the fun ticket (aka money).

Go back in time when modern problems weren't an issue, no real bills such as electricity, gas, telephone, child care and so forth, and then add in eBay, credit cards, cell phones and all the financial $$$ for "survival" of today. However did they do it? The closest thing people had in the old days to a cell phone was a homing pigeon, and your credit card was begging for a bit of bread and promising something in return, and for your troubles you might have promptly hightailed it out of the village before you were caught or at the least kicked all over the village common.

So let's go back to that time for a bit. Winter is coming so you stock up on food, bring in the harvest and feed up the cows, sheep, goats, fowl and such to get them through the winter. You will need to slaughter the beasts that will not survive the cold as they are already weak and then preserve the meat for the dark months ahead and waste nothing. Feathers are used for warmth in quilts; the hide and the wool of the slaughtered beasties are used for all sorts of things for survival. The tendons and sinew become thread, fat for oil lamps, hooves boiled down for glue of a sort, poop is a good filler for gaps in the wall and also for burning in the fire (nothing better than the smell of burning poop at dinnertime). Or here's a good one, instead of waking up to the aroma of coffee and fresh baked bread on a lazy Sunday, it's smoldering poop, a cupful of water from the well or creek, or some ale if the water isn't good, and whatever you can scrounge to eat, then off to the field you go to work your guts out the same as is done every single day. Nothing was wasted those days from crops to animals, you worked from dawn to dusk; every bit of daylight was used.

Consequently it was very unlike today as we waste everything, including personal time with friends and family and most importantly with ourselves. We might rather go out and spend heaps of money on getting drunk each and every weekend, when sometimes it's better to have a day or night at home to reflect on yourself and what you want to accomplish, than disguise an unfilled life with wasting valuable time.

For a first gathering if you can't find someone to go with, pick a lighter gathering such as Yule or a family spring/summer festival. The way to get to where you want to go is to make a plan and stick with it. Find yourself a piggy bank, jar, tin or whatever is handy to save your cents in, even a special bank account. Feed it on a regular basis each day if possible with any change you might have. Chuck in a little each week and it builds up. Planning ahead makes it so much easier. If you leave it to the last minute you may fail in your purpose. Actually all will fail unless you have a cash cow, money tree, or have just scored yourself a bit of a windfall. You will need to take into account, travel expenses, money for on the road, nutritious things like snacks, or chewy sweets that are bad for you, stopping off for a toilet break and a burger, and not least petrol money if you are going with someone else. It's an unwritten rule to share petrol expenses if you have managed to scrounge a lift. You will also spend money if there is a market day, a booze or cigarette run, or you might have forgotten something — your toothbrush for example, so it's off to the nearest town or village. On a rare occasion it's also an idea to have access to money to get you home again but only if you are such a pain in the proverbial to travel with, or you behave so badly at the gathering that you get the boot and are told to start walking.

On The Prowl, How to Spot a Pagan

Actually sometimes prowling can be difficult but as you develop your senses it gets easier and can be fun. Here are a few pagan spotting ideas to keep in mind.

Many pagans wear a talisman whether it is a necklace, bangle, brooch or some sort of jewelry. Some pagan's are easily spotted because they wear a printed T-shirt such as "Pagan and Proud of it," actually when I was at the Australian Wicca

Conference in Healesville in 2007, one lovely lady wore a T-shirt that read "P**s Off — if I wanted to know you, I would read your entrails." A definite witch I would say. Just you to let you know, Goths are not always pagan or witches, actually some of the world's most well-known witches look just the same as everyone else. I have my own two pet Goths (very Goth). They scared me a bit when I first saw them at the conference (I hadn't been too exposed to Goths before), anyway I walked into the room we were sharing and I didn't know what to expect. They turned out to be the nicest, caring, loving, understanding and gentle girls you would care to meet. I formed a strong friendship with the two girls who liked to dress in a certain way, as many of us like to dress as an individual.

It's funny the reaction the Goth girls received when the three of us went to the shop to do some hunter-gathering of food and booze supplies, they looked lovely, very gothic and witchy. Me...I tagged along in very girly shades of pink, the look on people's faces as they backed off, was classic — a mixture of fear and curiosity. I had one man come up to find out if I needed rescuing from the demon worshippers. I promptly told him that you do not judge a book by its cover and that I was the devil worshipper and these girls rescued me and had shown me the light of Jesus. Well, the guy could have competed in the hundred yard dash at the Olympics; he was out of there with a grayish tinge to his face, leaving us laughing until our ribs hurt.

As you get out and about you will become more attuned and find the instinct that is within you; it's like a sixth sense. You will be able to sniff out a pagan like a drug dog at the airport. Of course when you are at a gathering you will see a varied and marvelous assortment of clothes, many of the girls go for the medieval look, and I have seen a few wizards about, it's not compulsory, wear what you want, it's just a bit of fun and adds to the atmosphere.

Now onto the easier pagan spotting techniques, as I said most but not all pagans wear a talisman of some sort. The pentacle or pentagram are well known but even these can be disguised, so look closely when you see a symbol that looks familiar, yet doesn't. There are many, many symbols, such as the triquetra, triple moon, a goddess symbol, dragons, faeries, and so on. Different faiths have different symbols, such as a Norse practitioner might have Thor's hammer, or a double-sided axe. Look up symbols on Google it's very interesting.

I wear a black obsidian ring on my ring finger, but on my right hand a small pentacle and an aqua aura crystal, as well as three bangles, one from my coven, one from a druid priestess, and a third of hematite. When I am at a gathering or somewhere special I will wear a fancier pentagram or a dragon which stand out. I've seen some very interesting jewelry such as carved crystal, bones, spheres with herbs inside, and some I don't recognize, so I look up what it represents later, or ask the wearer if it is a symbol of anything specific. If you do this too you are guaranteed one of two reactions, the *fob off-go away reaction*, respect this and back off, you don't want to be turned into something that lives down a drain pipe and eats sludge. Luckily and more usually the wearer will tell the story behind it. The more you let them know how interested you are, the more they will loosen up and probably be more than happy to share their particular knowledge with you, now they know you are one of them. And *voila* a new friend has been made.

Other things to look for are car stickers. I have a sticker that says "my other car is a broom." People's homes give a lot away, especially their book collection, decorations, or an altar in disguise (or not), it's just a case of looking and seeing. There are two different ways of looking, you can look but not see and see without looking.

Good luck prowling. Oh and I nearly forgot, when you are getting together your own symbol, clothes, or whatever, whether you make them yourself or buy them, have fun, these make you unique and you also become one of the prowled, as well as a prowler.

Just a Quick Rave

Something I will guarantee you is that within a year of attending workshops, get-togethers and/or gatherings, you will have a section in your wardrobe that will include at least one cloak of some description and a collection of "special" clothes that are worn only when you are out and about with your magical friends. I also know people that wear the same clobber all the time. It's up to you. Me...I do a bit of both. I have my full on witchy velvet type dresses and cloaks, but I also have some witchy tops that I wear occasionally in the non-pagan realm as well. Generally I keep my clothes separate, for one thing it's easier to pack when I'm off on some adventure and it's symbolic of leaving the day to day drudge behind. I do not go overboard, and just have clothes that I like and feel comfortable in but different from my usual uniform or mundane same-as-everyone-else type stuff. Unlike the non-pagan realm, no one cares about being seen in the same outfit. It's actually a good thing as you can be spotted in a large crowd because of your own unique style. It's also good because when you get something new you are fawned over and complimented on the fabulous addition to your "special" wardrobe collection.

People wear varied clothes such as full on witchy-poo garb all weekend, Goth-type clothing, general day clothes, and amazingly time-consuming, hand-sewn, medieval re-enactment clothes to bright, tie-dyed, hippy type clothes. It doesn't matter and everyone does actually look as if they fit in.

Something happens that really can't be explained when you attend a gathering or even day workshops. I call it the veil. I have been to many workshops and gatherings, and after a couple of hours I feel the veil come over us cloaking us from the outside and keeping us wrapped in our own world for the duration.

When everyone leaves and you yourself are on your way home back to the day-to-day world you will feel it lift, so basically wear what is comfortable for you everything and anything is accepted.

Dressing up, particularly on feast night, is fun and is the night everyone looks forward to, even the guys get themselves spruced up. I have seen some elaborate costumes, and some amazing and colorful body art. My particular favorite is the morning wear, a few people are dressed already by breakfast but most of us just like to slide into the day and trudge around for a while in our pajamas. I get a new pair for each gathering but the breakfast fashion show is a great hoot seeing who's wearing what, from elegant silk to bright flannelette to something borrowed from the night before. To start the day like that has got to be beneficial apart from being a giggle. Over a coffee and when your sight is not so blurry from just waking up, you might notice the panda eyes or streaked paint and the lipstick that is spread across the left side of someone's face. Don't forget the bed head hairdo as some of these can be quite scary in addition to the streaked make-up, and is worthy of spitting up your cereal as you nearly choke from laughing. It's only when you go back to your cabin to clean yourself up, you discover that you yourself could have come from a B grade horror movie.

Skyclad?
Now onto the Skyclad thing that everyone wants to know about. Not every ritual, gathering or get-together, is in jiggly-wobbly, naked mode. Myth buster — most skyclad ceremonies/rituals are in private with a coven or select group of friends who are trusted experienced practitioners and members, and seldom in public view.

It would not be a good idea to go straight to a skyclad ritual, unless you were bought up in a naturist colony. It can be quite confronting for anyone, observers are not welcome in most cases especially dodgy ones, and most people don't like someone standing in the trees looking at their jiggly-wobbly bits. So before you go to any rituals or public or more private gatherings, read about it, check out all the information first and contact organizers to ask questions.

If you are happily going to a skyclad event, it doesn't necessarily mean you are naked all the time, but this will be mentioned on your welcome pack. The benefit is you also don't have to pack so much stuff. I have found that taking a sarong or light cover such as a wrap is accepted till the ritual begins, so if you are feeling a bit awkward you are covered to a degree until the time comes when the skin becomes the only required covering. This might be a bit nerve wracking at first but once you are in ritual you won't notice, then later you can pick up the wrap and cover yourself if you so wish.

If you are planning to go to an event that states that clothing is optional (these events are more often on private property), there are still a few niceties to follow and a bit of discretion should be used. You might be fine waltzing around in your skin, but there will be others there that will be clothed because they are uncomfortable with their own skin, or will only go naked for the ritual. For whatever reason it may be, you need to be considerate of them and don't go flouncing your jiggly-wobbly bits all over the place.

A friend told me of just such an event that had workshops with an international guest so they really wanted to go, but what ruined it for them and others were a particular skyclad couple who would sit with the clothed folk and reach across the table to fetch something. This being rude in the first place, was unpleasant for others at a table that didn't particularly like boobs dangling in their food or to have some blokes "boy pack" against their elbow as he tried to get past, so be thoughtful and discreet. Most pagans don't mind skin but there is a time and place and expected behavior.

Do not go into this lightly, make sure you are comfortable with the others in the circle and follow your instinct and ask yourself, "Am I ready for this?"

Accessories

A dear friend of mine made me a small bag that has since become decorated with all sorts of odds and ends and dingly bling. I use it to cart around cigarettes, a portable ash tray, notebook, and a pencil and camera. Most people do have some sort of bag they take with them for essentials. You really do not need all the bits and pieces you have crammed into your day-to-day bag. Generally, it's not a good idea to take valuables and if the organizers don't have a safe place (which is usually the case), then lock them in the boot of your car.

Tips (gained the hard way)

I am really good at this pagan lark and I can tell you I am still learning — new mistakes that is! I am sure I will get around to learning from them at some stage, but most of my friends think this is highly unlikely. I personally think they are the instigators and just like to watch me put my foot in it or laugh at me as I go squirreling looking for unintended mischief. Though I have come up with some very inventive saving graces and on the odd occasion someone else got the blame, but this is rare. So be organized and maybe think first as you never know when you might come across the aforementioned friends and you too will be slapped with the silly stick. They are not particular, they must be sick of slapping me by now, so your turn it is unless you take note of the *slappy* avoidance wisdom I am about to impart. Now that you are getting out and about, there are few tricks that will hopefully save you some blood, sweat and tears, as well as wasted time, an injured neck, back, or the whole aching skin wrapped pain receptacle, lack of sleep, wasting money and so on. Freezing or sweltering in your own skin bag can be unpleasant too.

First of all you have to be organized. If you are going to a gathering or event, read all the fine print on your welcome pack, research your destination but also the site itself and how you are going to get there and back. Have a plan B just in case something goes wrong, and check out the weather before you go. Ask the organizers questions. There is no question too silly except for the one that wasn't asked and you can bet that will be the one that bites you. The information here is mainly for weekend gatherings and events but also day workshops. Even if you live close to the site, it is a good idea to pack with thought for the day/s as you don't want to miss anything, and if others find out you are going on a hunter-gatherer expedition because you forgot something, you could be gone until it's time to pack up. I only did this once and learnt very quickly. I now take extra items just in case.

You will gradually learn who the habitual forgetters are and it will be your decision how to deal with them and whether you wish to help or not. People more often than not come under the description of either the "help pixie" or "no-help horror." Either will make their presence and attitude known very quickly, so be cautious. The first offer of help you make to the *black hole* type person could well become an expected and frequent behavior. This can also be at your own expense, either personally or financially, as the habitual *black hole* people won't stop asking for help in most instances and the user/supplier relationship quickly wears thin. What I am trying to say is make sure you have everything you need and it's also perfectly fine to share if you know the person is not a sponge, otherwise point them towards the nearest hunter-gather facility.

So now let's move onto some face-saving and space-saving tips to help you prepare for your trip. I have included ideas that I think are important and hopefully save you a bit of grief. Remember to check the weather, plan your clothing and put them near the bag you are taking (give and take as the weather can change suddenly so take things that you can layer and take off as the day gets warmer). In the colder months, I take one set of cool clothes along with the woolens so if there happens to be freak warm weather you have the right clothing and won't swelter. In the warmer weather treat it the other way around and take a warm jacket.

I bought myself a sheet-size polar fleece and cut a line halfway down the middle. This can then be worn as a warm wrap and can also used as a blanket on the bed or even a blanket on the ground. They are also good to tuck under the top bunk to give you a bit of privacy and keeps out the light and some of the noise made by the stragglers bumps and thumps as they crawl or stagger back to the bunk house you are all sharing.

I always take my own pillow even though several sites provide pillows. Some are good but some the devil designed for drooling or greasy-haired boy and girl Scouts and you never know what disease riddled youth germs are festering in there.

Mattresses can be the same but lumpier or have the famous Scout body indentation and also the history about what the little *'tweenteen* did there too. So besides taking your own pillow, as far as getting something half-decent where the mattress department is concerned, you need to arrive as close to opening as possible. Even better, arrive early to help set up, that way you also get a chance to test out mattresses and pick your space. Swap mattresses if you can. Making your claim by leaving a bit of paper with your name on it does not work. Stake a full claim by making your bed with your sleeping bag or sheets and blankets, and having your suitcase nearby. Putting some stuff on top of bed helps prove ownership too.

Once done, you can go off to be the *help pixie*, this way if there is a dispute about bed space you have organizers as allies and your stuff is neatly in place which means ninety percent of the law of ownership. It rarely fails. There's always, "I was here first" and as a whole it is accepted practice that the first to arrive has first choice of bed.

While you are doing your *help pixie* duties, talk to all the others and soak up every bit of information you can about what's happening over the weekend. Don't forget to ask names and remember them if you are sent on gopher duty. Explore the site as well to find where everything is and inspect the general layout, this is called basic reconnaissance. You can go and have a longer look later, but at least for now you will have a general idea of where to go.

Something else that is likely to happen while you are fumbling around watching the experts as they claim the best spot in minutes, is that you will hear some great stories of bed horrors that have been endured, but also about fabulous sites that have the newest and latest luxury (that is Scout luxury, not hotel luxury). Unless you are at one of the upper market events or retreats usually the same site is used again and again so eventually you will get to know places well. You in turn will be telling your stories in the future to the ones that will come to you with the same questions, call it the *wheel of memories*. You will have a giggle to yourself and think how that was you all that time ago, thus producing empathy hormones and now it is your turn and you will do your best to guide and educate the little bird that you once were.

Travel: When traveling it is an idea to make a list that you can leave in your bag or pocket and if you forget something add it to the list and then for future reference you just haul out the list and you can be packed in minutes. If you are traveling you have to be really clever in mix and match clothes and what you can fit in your bag to get away with excess luggage if you're flying. If your bag is heavy, be brutal and dump a few items or take some items as hand luggage.

Medications: Don't forget to take any medications that you will need. To save space, buy a plastic medication box or put any medication in clearly labeled re-sealable plastic bags, and include a small basic first aid kit. Don't forget the mosquitoes at night so take ample protection spray and antihistamine cream in case you are bitten by any insects. Band Aids should be included too.

Cosmetics: Collect small bottles before the trip to use for your toiletries and these are possibly the heaviest of our essentials. You won't need a full-size bottle of shampoo for just three days, but you would be surprised at the amount of times I have seen this and they just end up being ditched. There are solid shampoos and conditioners which don't weigh anywhere near as much as liquid. You can buy these online. Ear plugs are a must and I also take a small bottle of antiseptic spray. I have stayed in some dubious places that have had stains that look as if they belong in a forensic laboratory.

Weather: Check the weather carefully and if unsure about it take a mixture of warm and cool clothes and remember no-one cares if you wear the same thing all weekend. To suit the weather if it is warm, still take at least one long-sleeved top and a jacket just in case. For cooler weather wear clothing that is layered as you can take items off when inside. Don't forget something for if it rains. You can buy plastic ponchos from travel shops that weigh nothing and fold into a tiny bag. Also think about what you are going to wear to feast nights and such. You can stay scruffy and in the same clothes all weekend but make feast night special as it really does make a difference to dress up and be clean and neat. You don't have to wear pagan ceremonial clothes just something you feel comfy in and looks fine too.

Footwear: I usually take a pair of jogging shoes and a pair of plain slip-ons. Wellington/galoshes are also a must for bad weather. This all depends on the weather and the organizers who know the site will usually give you an idea of what to wear as well, as they have walked over the place long beforehand.

Bedding: I always take my own pillow, sheets and my polar fleece blanket. All of these don't take up as much room as a sleeping bag. This is where the antiseptic spray comes in. I spray the mattress and quilt for no other reason than I don't know what yukky little Boy Scout body has been there before me. If the bedding is a bit musty, spraying it makes it smell that much fresher. And don't forget to pick your bed carefully you could have to put up with the mattress from hell all weekend. Bed hunting, testing and claiming is a legitimate part of the experience.

Miscellaneous: Though I have never had the time, I take a book to read just in case. I also take a pen and notepad in a plastic sleeve. I put all my handouts from the workshops in the sleeve to keep them together until I get home. If you are asked to bring something specific to a workshop, put it with your stationary bundle.

To protect anonymity, if you take photographs of individuals don't forget to ask permission and never publish them later on the internet or anywhere else for that matter unless you have asked first.

Some people take their iPods for when there is free time, but do not turn it up so loud that it can be heard outside your earphones. Some people just want to hear the quiet sounds of nature without some heavy metal maniac in the background.

Take a portable ashtray if you smoke. Talking of which don't forget to pack enough cigarettes to get you through, along with snacks and alcohol as sometimes there are no stores nearby (not that I'm advocating smoking, drinking or eating junk food).

Don't forget to take a torch, a small one will do. I have never needed one of those torches that light up an area of a kilometer and can be seen from space. Most places have reasonable lighting as they are usually Scout camps or places where the public stay. If you at a camping site though, it is a must. It's good to have one handy as when you are going into your cabin or room, people may be asleep. You can use your torch to find your bed and to prevent putting on your pajamas inside out or back to front without disturbing the others. What are you doing staying out so late anyway?

A small pouch or shoulder bag is handy to take too. You don't want to be carrying a handbag or rucksack around the place filled with stuff you won't need. Better to lock it in the boot of yours or a friend's car.

Workshops, ritual and meal times if applicable will be given in your welcome pack. As far as meals go if you are late you will get cold or overcooked food. You should also be given workshop times too. These are allocated for a reason, so don't be late and get into the "pagan time" mind frame. If you are late for a workshop you not only disrupt the others but could well have missed out on some crucial information. If one workshop is delayed it just puts the others behind or one of them will have to be shortened.

Something you should consider are events that have overlapping workshops or ones that have a time clash, so you will need to decide which holds your interest more Mark your timetable so you can plan your time and know where you have to be.

Sometimes you are asked to bring something for a workshop, so if you are not sure what that is, just ask and the speaker can tell you exactly what you need and probably where to get it.

Some speakers supply everything you need and it really is not a good idea to improvise. I was once off to a fire-twirling workshop and before we were allowed to even go near the fire we had to practice with homemade poi made with stockings that had tennis balls inside. I couldn't be bothered going to the shops and buying stockings and balls so I improvised with an old pair of tights and two hockey pucks. Off I went to the workshop happy with my inventiveness. This alone should have screamed warnings at me. Anyway halfway through the exercise we had already greatly improved and people were twirling around at the speed of light, until all hell broke loose and my pucks became missiles on a mission of destruction. The poi instructor dropped like a bag of sand clutching at his boy bits and with a really strange color to his face. The other heat seeking missile hit some poor person on the head. When my victims were released from hospital, I was given the news that thankfully both would fully recover. So the moral to that story is to follow instructions. My instructions are to stay away from poi, and after burning down the pergola I actually do agree with this.

It shouldn't be too long now before you are out and about, and this should make it all a bit easier. There will still be things that you can screw up or mischief to get into and new tricks to learn that make the whole gathering or event experience an experience to remember. It is completely up to you what you put into it and what you take out as long as you try not to damage anything or anyone in the process.

Pagans and Dis-abilites

Yep! Even we magical people have the same chances as everyone else of being born with a defect sticker or having an accident or illness that also requires a defect sticker whether it is short or long term. As far as illness goes, do not go anywhere if you are sick with some bug that can spread. If it is another sort of illness it might be an idea to find out where the nearest medical facility is and by what means are you going to get there in an emergency. From what I have seen before, and after being given the defect notice myself, it doesn't matter and we are welcomed and treated as everyone else. That does not mean it's a free ride and if you expect everyone to look after you, think again, it will not happen as you are too high maintenance. People do not pay to go to events to spend their time playing unplanned slave or nurse maid. If you are high maintenance person bring a carer with you. If you just generally need a bit of a hand it is not a problem but you also will be expected to do what you can do to help in return.

Let's go through the possible hurdles.

Accommodation can be tricky as most gatherings are at camps or similar and most day workshops are held at community halls or schools and even the private getaways at retreats. These days though pretty much all of them make allowances for disabilities. When you fill out your registration form you may have to tell the organizers what the affliction is and what special needs you may have such as special diet, wheelchair access, a need to be located near to the toilet, or that you walk with a stick or sticks. This way they can make sure you are bedded down somewhere appropriate for your needs so you can get around all right. This does not always go to plan, so if you find where you are staying is not suitable then talk to the hosts and see if they will sort you out. Do your research beforehand to see if it is right for you before you decide to go

Just after I ditched my crutches and still wasn't walking

properly, I went to a gathering and found accommodation on ground level, but the hall, ritual site and workshop area, were either up or down stairs. What's more, my bed was the top bunk as the other beds were already claimed. It was simply a case of talking to the organizer and finding my bunk buddies to explain the situation and the problem was solved.

Another thing to check when you are researching the site is the terrain, and as most gatherings are out in the boondocks the terrain can be a challenge.

Traveling can also be tricky, particularly if you are catching a ride with someone you don't know well as you will need to look at your capability of getting in and out of the car and what sort of equipment if any that you require, as space will be limited. It's not fair to let someone be squished in a corner because you have extra stuff, so warn them beforehand. What about public transport? For this you really need to be fairly independent and check out how far you will have to go to get to the event as it really is a case of being well-informed and organized long before you plan to go or even apply to go. So check out all your options first.

Rituals, whether it be a simple full moon ritual, or one of those fabulous rites at a gathering with heaps of people, there's no reason why you can't go just because you have a disability. I think the main thing would again be the location and what the terrain is like. As for the ritual itself there are two choices, either sit on the sidelines or when it gets too much for your capabilities step back for a while. If it is an accepted practice, then rejoin the circle when you are able. Both these options do not exclude you from energy raising or enjoying yourself. You can become an enthusiastic spectator and share energy, cheering the more able-bodied as they go screaming past at great velocity with the G force of nine at the tail-end of a spiral dance.

The Help Pixie might be there to help you if you are not capable of helping and doing your fair share. Make sure you bring her/him/them with you or that someone or more than one person has volunteered to help. Do not use your disability as an excuse not to join in there will be something that you can do. Other people will respect your effort for being there even if you cannot physically help.

Mental Health Issues is a sensitive subject and I was in two minds about including it as it is open to controversy. I do think it's a subject that should be covered so I will apologize now as it is not my intention to upset anyone.

Mental health is a subject that not long ago was taboo but over the past decade has become an accepted and more understandable illness. Just as with a physical disability a mental disability is one that should be catered for. The most important thing is your responsibility for yourself. If you don't take your medication and become psychotic you will be removed, also any form of self-harm while at an event will not be tolerated and more than likely you will be put on the blacklist for future events. It's not the responsibility of the organizers or the guests to keep an eye on you or to remind you to take medication. Some behavior will be tolerated to a certain extent as people will empathize with your condition, but the line is thin. It might be an idea to talk to one of your support people to ask them if they think you are mentally stable enough to go to an event, as you know sometimes you yourself do not see when you are becoming unwell. Hopefully your support person will be honest with you so you can then get appropriate help as a gathering or event is not the place to have a psychotic episode.

I have been to an event where one of the guests was suffering from Tourette's Syndrome the organizers were pre-informed so were prepared to discreetly handle any issues that arose. However, someone that is on the verge of a psychotic episode is another issue all together and there are few people that know how to deal with the issue and should not even be put in that situation. When applying for an event, do give organizers a detailed account of your mental health issues and medications. It would also be a good idea to mention anything that triggers an episode, or signs to look for when you are starting to become unwell. If the organizers feel they are unable to handle the situation, you may be asked not to go to a certain event for your own safety as well as their own and the guests. So please understand that it is for no other reason other than insurance and most importantly your welfare.

Children are another subject. If you have a child with a physical or mental disability or even without one, remember that it is *you* who are responsible for that child. If the child disrupts other guests, during workshops or rituals you may well be asked to leave. Far more preferable is to take children where you know they are welcome and the rituals allow for them. At some events, there are even activities arranged especially for the children. These events in general tend to be less informal and the odd crying child is fine, but not the one who tries to jump the fire or go for a midnight swim in the pond and has to be rescued. Keep an eye on them at all times.

Harmonia on Pagan Camps

Camps can be of any size and located anywhere from someone's garden to covering two or three fields. The smaller camps are more often private rituals.

You obviously need camping equipment. This can vary from just a tent and sleeping bags as food is provided, to the whole kit and caboodle.

The whole kit and caboodle will consist of tent (an awning is a nice extra), sleeping bags, water cans or bottles, camping stove and gas bottle, or cauldron and charcoal, picnic plates and cutlery, folding chairs and table, easy to cook food, drinks, aluminum foil (for baked potatoes if cooking on a fire), torches, toilet paper (just in case you don't know who'll be cooking), washing-up bowl, cloth/scourer, washing-up liquid, and pots and pans. You will also need the usual personal items and many things that Kimi has mentioned in *Tips* above.

Get to the camping area early to ensure you have enough space to park your 4 x 4 vehicle and put up your three-roomed luxury tent with separate dining area, large awning and room for a pony. Even with our one room, no awning basic tent, it was a struggle to find space.

Harmonia Saille

Be prepared for chilly weather. On a camp I went to in the UK at the end of a bad summer, it was ridiculously chilly at night. The first night there neither we nor any of our friends slept, as we were too cold. The next night we were better prepared. Having struggled the night before with our sleeping bags and getting in a right tangle, we decided to open them up and use them as blankets. We had brought a duvet with us so put that on top and we slept in our clothes and low and behold we slept all night. We found that our friends had gone to bed wearing extra clothes and had also slept well.

Be prepared for the weather. Waterproofs and boots are a must if bad weather is expected or there has been lots of recent rain. Tramping around in cold mud in your best sandals is no fun nor is trench foot. Remember, it's a camping trip not a fashion show (except when the weather allows, then many of us are out in our best frocks or outfits), so in bad weather dress to suffer less, not to impress! Best take lots of dry socks too and an extra towel if rain is expected. Another good extra is to take a warm blanket for chilly nights to wrap around you while sitting around the fire or cauldron singing, "We all come from the goddess."

A good cauldron can be useful when filled with barbeque charcoal to provide warmth and you can also cook on it if necessary. It will also take small pans or alternatively wrap potatoes in foil and bake.

If you can find someone to share cooking facilities with, it can save buying your own stove. We shared cooking facilities with friends, and were lucky to be camped close by. On the last day they were leaving before us, but it's surprising who you can find to cook you bacon and eggs…even a complete stranger (but wait to be invited, don't just randomly march into your next door neighbor's camp demanding for your bacon sandwich to be made). Though as the others packed up they did point fingers and accuse us of defecting as they spotted us at someone else's table.

Toilets can be a nightmare. Queues are inevitable at the portaloos (portable toilets). We were lucky at our last festival that there was also a toilet block. Do not expect the toilets to be as clean on the last day as they were on the first as it can get particularly nasty in there. Advice here is please leave the toilet clean. Guys please learn how to hit into the toilet bowl not next to it! Parents please make sure your kids flush. Lastly do not leave any bits of soggy toilet paper hanging around that you used to dry your hands on. Every little helps. There was a tap for fresh water in one of the fields at the large event I was at, but this might not always be the case at all gatherings, so ask beforehand and take bottled water if necessary.

At the bigger gatherings, there are usually marquees for the workshops, and space set aside for other activities.

Take your litter home with you, or put it in the bins if provided and recycle if possible.

Do not take alcohol unless your welcome pack says it is allowed and generally abide by the rules.

There is a check list for this chapter at the back of the book.

2

Kimi's Guide to Ethics, Etiquette, Boobs and Bums

Code of Conduct

This article can be considered "Occupational Health and Safety." Not only is it your safety but the safety of others.

The one and only thing to remember if nothing else is if it doesn't feel right, don't do it, don't go there, don't watch it, don't be there and don't listen to it. Run away, go, depart, leave, and be discreet if you can. If you are okay with what's going on until a certain point, then discreetly stand back. Again you should have been informed about what's happening before it does actually happen, so it's a case of listen carefully or read the small print if you get a flyer for a certain event or gathering and make an informed decision. Don't make one of those decisions that you think is all right until you decide it's not all right. Think carefully.

In some circumstances, if you behave badly or with disrespect, even pretending to know more than you actually do, and annoying others with this so-called knowledge, you will be caught out. You could be smelling de-composed wombat carcass for many years to come and get yourself a reputation which will ultimately lead to a solitary existence. No one will invite you to anything; even your application to attend an event could be turned down. The community on a whole is fairly tolerant but you still need to watch your manners as you would in everyday life. The community is also relatively small so word gets around quickly.

The code of conduct is not just yours but what you should

expect and receive from others. This code of conduct especially includes experienced practitioners and long-standing community members who should not only be more attuned with your status and make allowances for it, but should also inform and watch over you.

At most events whether it is a weekend gathering or a simple full moon ritual you will may well be "buddied" (someone will be assigned to look out for you), even without you realizing it. Something to remember is there may be other (new to the community) people and their conduct should be taken into account and if you feel uncomfortable with a certain person's behavior, whether they are a newbie or not, talk to your buddy or the host organizers (I propose a new word for "newbie" to the community, how about "hatchling?").

When you receive your welcome pack to a gathering or event you will more than likely receive a list of rules too. Read it carefully and follow instructions.

Another point to remember is not to touch other people's belongings especially their magical items. By this stage you should know what that is, but sometimes a magical item might just look like a roughly polished stick, a crude bit of metal that resembles a knife, or an old cup. Not all tools are obvious, but even someone's ritual cloak should be considered off limits as it might have a special meaning to that person. Musical instruments, drums, flutes, bells and so forth are also in the *no-go* basket. To be safe don't touch anything unless you are invited to.

You might come upon a wand, chalice, and stones or crystals that look as if they were just left outside in some random place. Do not assume the owner just left them behind, they could have been placed there for the purpose of charging or cleansing by moon or sun. Even partied up pagans usually keep a close watch on their things, so don't assume or you could have angry pagan on your tail. Most people will be happy to show you and explain the history of the interesting article you just want to get your sweaty little paws on and ogle over.

At most gatherings I have attended, the important "no touch" stuff is wrapped or bagged as most folk know if they leave a wand or athame hanging around it will more than likely be handled. The thing to do if you want to handle something is to just ask. From asking you will get one of three responses, " No, go away, touch and die" or "yes, look but don't touch as it has been charged" but the more usual is "sure maul it all you want," but then you are trapped into listening to the full version of the items history and creation and be subject to the gloat factor (hunter-gather code of conduct). If this happens to you, be polite and listen though this can get hard after several hours of raving and you will be bored out of your mind and wished you never had the *curiosity-touch-drool* thoughts in the first place.

So the moral is every action has an equal and possible opposite reaction. Don't touch working tools especially if they are inside a circle and never throw anything into a cauldron unless specifically asked as you will get an evil look (if you are lucky), more than likely you'll be cursed then turned into a sludge-sucking slime creature. Alternatively, if you are at a gathering you could become the victim of bunk bed sabotage and personally I'd rather have a smack around the head than have my bed messed with. There are so many possible reprisals from this action and none of them are good after a long day of workshops.

I have only been involved with a few espionage bed tortures and that is all I am going to say about that for fear of recrimination. I know firsthand what can be done but we had fun doing it. The victim didn't get much sleep though.

Apart from the fun stuff, be respectful and exactly like you want to be respected back. Respect not just your property but yourself as a worthy person of the group. Use your instinct of when to talk and when to listen. In a circle, just listen as you will need to know what's going on, and (I know I've said this before) do not be so rude as to whisper to your friend standing next to you, especially if the rite is underway as concentration is needed. Having some numbnuts squeaking away will wreak havoc on the energy control. If you need to ask questions about the ritual, do so beforehand and preferably ask one of the members hosting it, as the priest/ess will be psyching up and preparing themselves. They do not need the distraction. If you are at all unsure about the ritual, then simply observe until you feel comfortable with the group then you can join in wholeheartedly next time.

When you are in a social situation if someone either has an opinion you don't like or agree with, then be quiet or present your view in a logical, educated and nice manner and be prepared to backup your statement. Make sure you know your facts and remember that opinions are just that, opinions. In quite a few cases you are saying the same thing just in different words.

Sit back and listen to others as there can be some very interesting and informative, sometimes heated, debates. Times like this are actually a good time to stay quiet, to listen and be educated, as you hear the views and thoughts of others. You can decide later what you thought suited you best. You could also track down the person later for a one on one conversation. Do not interrupt them if they are engaging in meditation, contemplation or if they look as if their thoughts are elsewhere. Do not worry as you will learn body language as you develop your intuitive skills.

At a ritual, gathering or day workshop, actually anywhere not just pagan but any circle you are walking in, say having dinner at a friend's house, your parents, or at a workplace, wherever you may be, offer to help. Be prepared to work. Sometimes people say yes so don't just offer and walk away thinking they will be all right, you might be thrown in the deep end with a reply of "great!" and asked to start washing, collecting, or serving. This can be an advantage as you will get to meet people in real life, not just reading book after book. Getting out there to mingle with real people in a situation you are new to can be a bit scary, but you can bond while you are elbow deep in dish washing. I met some of my best friends during our turn at being dish washer. So do offer your assistance to the hosts, be a pack horse and help carry things to and fro, be a gopher for sending their messages. Your offer of help may be accepted or not but the fact you asked counts for much. It's a well known fact in the community that it's always the same people that help out, it's also known who the ones are that don't. If you were at a friend's house you would offer assistance, so do so at gatherings and events. Many events ask for volunteers upfront so you can offer your services and be told what you will be doing in advance.

Getting on With People and Gossip

I have touched on this a bit earlier but due to a recent "upheaval" in my community I want to just add a bit more and remind you that though the country you live in may seem large, the community you are now part of is very close-knit and word travels quickly even from country to country and continent to continent. You will come across some people that get into the politics and want things done their way or no way. Things from the non-pagan realm leak in, and of course it is human nature anyway to believe that we are right and that's all there is to it. Sometimes we are not right though and this is where we sit back and listen to the views and opinions of others, and form our own opinion. It might be an idea to keep that opinion to yourself at the moment, and if you are a newbie it would be a very wise idea to just stay out of any political discussion until you have some knowledge and have experience behind, along with a good reputation of trust, knowledge and proven worthiness.

One of the biggest no-no's is gossip or repeating things you have heard. It's a big bad NO! Whether you are new to the community or not, it's a good ethic to take with you throughout your life whether it is in the pagan community or day-to-day world. All gossip does is destroy and hurt, whether you are a single person or a group or community. Hold your tongue and don't become involved. If you just can't help yourself go straight to the horse's mouth and ask them what it's all about so you hear both sides, and then still keep quiet. You may have come into a conversation that has been long standing, and so you don't know was going on. Walk away and don't get involved and certainly do not repeat whatever you heard. It's the same as in the non-pagan realm, things get lost in translation rather like in the game Chinese Whispers, and you never know if the gossip could be about you.

If you have a wagging tongue, you will develop a bad reputation and you will find yourself on the outer edge of the community. It doesn't take long to work out who can be trusted with information, think of the so-called Burning Times, one slip of the tongue would get some poor person barbecued so be careful as you could be the next sausage on the grill.

Etiquette

On skyclad etiquette, if you're new to skyclad events — unless you look like Adonis or Aphrodite — I would suggest your first one be at a same sex ritual if possible, and you should be able to find some "women only" events, especially for purposes of rites of passage. There are also "men only" events but I couldn't get much information on that as none of the guys were willing to talk. They must have taken the gossip section to heart and will not even give up just a snippet.

If you attend a ritual that is mixed or even same sex be sure you can go through with it to the end, as it is perfectly fine to step back if there is something you can't do (such as physical limitations). If you do need to stand back it will still be skyclad so don't go grabbing your cloak as you are still part of the circle.

Something else that is unacceptable for skyclad etiquette is not to openly look at other people's jiggly-wobblies. In many cases this will be furthest thing from your mind as a hundred kilos of wobble, or cemetery worthy skeleton dances by. If the dancing corpse rattles its bones right in front of you (yes just thinking about it conjures up an awful vision in your brain) it will probably damage you psychologically for many months to come.

As for the Adonis, who manfully rippling his muscles covered by perfect skin goes by with manly grace and animal prowess and indicates to you "look at me," all I can say is try not to do this. It will take every ounce of discipline you have and do not under any circumstances drool, or go glassy-eyed. The open-mouth thing, even a little bit, is a dead giveaway that you peeked. I can tell you from experience that you can also be punished by the gods. I didn't drool, just went into a fixed stare trance at the most unbelievable looking guy I have ever seen (but have not seen since thank the Goddess). I paid dearly with my dignity for my lapse in protocol because as I was absorbed in my own fantasy I somehow managed to unbalance and ended up in a well-placed mud hole and had to stay there until the circle had finished so I could be rescued. I can tell you as will others that it was not as sexy or erotic as mud-wrestling seems to be. In my case it was a much laughed about event that haunted me for months. I am now in a different country and it is still mentioned twenty years later, so be warned! This also goes for the guys ogling the Aphrodite types. Most of the time when you are in a ritual skyclad, you are too involved with the ritual to even think about such things but lapses do happen.

While we are on the skin subject I thought it important to mention some information on shared accommodation. At many gatherings you are not always put into same sex rooms, cabins or dormitories, so you could be sharing and more than likely you will not know anyone, especially if you are new to the community. In most cases the organizers will put you somewhere appropriate but if you do end up in a mixed sex room, be discreet. You can hang a cloak between bunk beds or get changed under your cloak or in the bathroom. Whatever way you choose to do it discretion is warranted.

Another thing about sharing bunk space is just that *space*, so don't go hogging all the available space with all your bits and pieces. Everyone has bits and pieces so keep it compact and tidy as you all need room to move around, and if someone has to get up in the night they don't want to be stumbling all over messy people's gear.

There has only been one place where caretakers did not frequent the site while we were there doing work, whatever it is that caretakers do. In nearly all circumstances where you are staying there will be non-pagan workmen around. If this is the case then be polite but basically leave them alone.

I experienced an unpleasant incident last year at a Beltaine gathering where a few of us were stalked for the weekend by the caretaker. Mr. Creepy already had the notion that we were there for some big sex fest and unbeknown to us at the time one of the female guests who was gay, flirted and flaunted outrageously thinking it was a bit of fun. Being the sort of man that obviously doesn't get much attention, he thought he was in guy heaven and must have thought anyone was easy game. Accordingly, he hung around and chatted to the females then singled out his choices that he then approached when they were alone or away from the group. He really did become a predator because he was given the wrong impression. I will not go into details but he was inappropriate in all his actions, by the way he spoke, things he did, and the over familiar sleight-of-hand, watching from behind trees and general waiting around corners. This became a harrowing weekend for some of us. So avoid the workers if possible and if you come across a Mr. Creepy tell the organizers.

While we are on the subject of the Mr. Creepy variety of person, it does sadden me to tell you that like all communities we have baddies too, so be aware and follow your instinct. Organizers cannot vet everyone that applies for a gathering and there are always new people. The sleazy types just get a whiff of a possible new hunting ground and go to the gathering for their own negative reasons. They are generally figured out quickly as they do not know about anything much but will listen and pick up random bits and pieces that a newbie might take as real, and then they spin their web. However, it is not just outsider predators that do this, there are pagans that are fully versed in their path but are dark, unethical, and they take advantage of any situation, the vulnerable and the gullible. I think it was last year that a couple of practitioners of the craft offered some teenagers all their dreams come true and the all they had to do was have *magick* sex with them. They were caught and were dealt with by the authorities but this is not always the case, as the predator is not reported for whatever reason, but if this happens to you please tell someone.

Gatherings are great fun as you will soon get to know but don't go overboard or over-indulge in alcohol to the point of beyond tipsy and being barely able to walk. This usually ends up in you chucking up your guts in front of your friends or on your friends. What's more, vomiting over someone's drum or other belongings is really asking for a swift kick into the next realm. At one gathering I went to many years ago in Scotland one of the young lads got so drunk that he was barely conscious. He got up in the early hours of the morning wanting to go to the bathroom for a quick pee, but the different surroundings didn't seem to enter his pickled brain, so he did what he had to do and stumbled back towards his bed. Unfortunately, when he thought he was lifting the toilet lid it was actually someone's bag. I never saw this guy again so he is either living as a dung beetle or was asked to remove himself from the community as a whole. If you get totally wiped out you will just end up feeling awful the next day and missing out on the activities planned and will be forced to listen and live with what you did and what you can't remember and pay the consequences.

Well, that about covers this subject, so be on your best behavior and take your manners and common sense with you into the pagan community.

3

Step with Kimi into the World of Magic and Discovery

This is what this book is all about, after reading all the books in the comfort of the non-pagan realm it's time to step into the world of magic and discovery, and embark on a whole new journey, meeting new friends, and expanding your heart, mind and spirit, and bringing forward everything you have read into real life.

Reading about a ritual or gathering is so different to actually being there. I think this is probably the scariest part of the journey especially if you are going somewhere alone. In a way this can be better because you are then *forced* to interact and I can promise you that when you get there you will wonder why you were so nervous about going along. By the end of the weekend or ritual you can pretty much guarantee that someone will take you under their wing, and you will make at least one friend. Some organizers will provide you with a buddy to acquaint you with what's going on and when and where. They should also get you settled in and perhaps introduce you to others if they have to go off and do some work. It won't take you long to adapt and it will probably be you ditching your buddy when your inner magnet kicks in and you attract likeminded people.

I actually had a similar experience at a gathering that the group I am part of recently held. I had met a woman from the Northern Territory online and talked her into coming to the gathering. She knew no one and it was her first gathering. About two hours into the gathering after we had claimed our sleeping space and got settled, she was off with a bunk buddy making new friends, and that was it for the weekend of our relationship, my services were no longer required. Unless you are some real weirdo weasel, everyone is treated as family. Even weirdo weasels get a chance but probably passed from person to person so everyone gets a stint at weasel sitting. Gatherings and workshops are hard work for the organizers so it is fun and easy for the guests, but it's the same principle as having a dinner party or get together with friends at your home and all the work is behind the scenes, so as you would at a friend's house, offer to help and by doing this you earn some good brownie points but you also get to meet other people that are really *in* the community.

Private events are fabulous not just because of the fun but because it's like a very tight-knit family getting together, preparing and then cleaning up. Talking about the event, having a giggle and feeling really good that you all had such a great time, even the worst tasks don't seem so bad when shared. I had one those moments just last weekend, someone ate something that didn't agree with them and had a bit of a chucky accident in the bathroom. So there was the hostess and I cleaning up, I volunteered for the yuk part and while I was on the floor, down the drain, and in the bowl, my lovely friend held my hair back and passed me the paper towel. It was like doing surgery with the nurse passing me the instruments, but I was gagging and giggling and she was trying very hard not to. We must have looked a strange sight accompanied by even stranger grunting and snorting noises. Not to be outdone, our audience was howling with laughter and giving suggestions how to make our job easier. We worked as a team and next time the roles will be reversed with us giving the *helpful* suggestions.

You will also have discovered something special, whatever direction or path you are taking, whether you are alone or with others. You still travel alone because only you can tread your path even if you have a friend with the same ideas as you. You can walk a similar path but not together and at the same time as each journey is personal and belongs to only you. Do not try to encourage others to keep up and do as you do, as you will not yet have the wisdom of time, guidance, practice or skills. You will in time so don't be too quick and just wish your life away because you *want it now*, be patient and it will come to you when you are ready. Doesn't that suck! You want to share your new found knowledge and joy and full moon experiences and the discovery of the goddesses and gods, plants and herbs, meditations, chants and magic and so forth, but *do not* share just yet, give yourself time to take it in, so you really understand and know what you are talking about or you will lose credibility.

Experience everything that you have discovered and understand the concepts and responsibilities that go with it. Let yourself be educated by others and educate yourself without spouting off about things you really don't understand, or you will sound like an utter moron to someone that could well know better. Silence is a good listener. Become a sponge and take in everything you can, formulate it to how it fits you. Of course talk and discuss issues with people who have the knowledge, ask questions, question yourself and listen and *hear* what is being said. I was going to say listen to the answers, but that's not correct because the answer belongs to the person saying it and might not fit with you so in that case it is all about opinion and observation. That's why you question yourself.

Remember there is no definite right answer, even discussing history or how to do a ritual for example, the information in the books you have read are the opinions and experiences of the writer and the information should be used as a guide. For instance, just say you attended a simple full moon ritual then asked each participant to write down what they experienced, what they thought of the ritual itself and how it was conducted, you would find that all comments were different.

What is a Ritual and Why Do We Do It?

On rituals, I am not going into full text book mode as you have probably read everything you can lay your hands on. For your ritual you are probably thinking about something deep and meaningful that's done at night hidden in the trees. However we are ruled by ritual every day. We get up in the morning, go to the toilet, eat some food, clean our teeth, get dressed and prepare for the day whatever that may be. Then there is school, work, housework, this is a ritual and is performed in a personal and specific way. It's not just the witches and pagans who have rituals for magic or specific reasons, churches of pretty much all denominations have the same elements as a Wiccan rite, here's how I see it:

- Open circle — Priest meets his flock (are they called a flock because they follow without thought as sheep do?).
- Call the quarters — The church has representatives of these too, a candle on the altar (fire), font used for blessings (water), incense to purify the air (air), flowers (earth), they are statues of Jesus or Mary and sometimes pictures of saints (representatives of the Gods and Goddesses).
- Chants, song, music, noise making, raising energy — Priest gives his sermon and everyone sings hymns. If you have ever been up at 4.30 am in the morning, on some television channels you will find the *media* evangelists putting on a show worthy of Broadway, but they certainly get the crowd going, now that is energy raising. They also conduct healing on stage where they induce a frenzy like trance, touch the afflicted on the forehead (third eye), then push them back to be caught by people behind them (the trust that comes with coven or trusted group you are with).
- Cakes and ale, closing circle, grounding — In the Catholic

Church you are given bread and red wine to represent the body of Christ and the blood he spilled. Other churches have an urn for tea and coffee and the ladies of the parish try to outdo each other with their scones, cakes and biscuits. The churchgoers mull around talking about the sermon (ritual), and just relaxing (grounding), then they go off do whatever they are going to do and if that's something bad then it's okay because the devil got into them, so all they have to do is ask for forgiveness and it is granted and *voila*, they can go and do it again. We as pagans on the other hand take responsibility for our own actions and have to be prepared for the consequences upon ourselves. Do wrong and expect a butt kicking from the universe. It's quite simple, give out anything negative and expect it right back in some form or other. I guess another and better known saying for that is, "do unto others as you will have done to you." This is basically the Wiccan Rede, but also others that are now placed under the pagan umbrella, such as Druid, Asatru, Dianic, Solitaries and so forth have their own wording, but it still means the same, take responsibility for yourself and what you do or suffer the consequences — simple!

Rituals

All rituals are different, for different reasons, seasons and occasions. A successful ritual depends on who writes and develops it. Those called to help as guardians, the elemental representatives, vessels of the Lady and Lord, even people in the circle for the first time are important to the outcome, energy and fulfillment. There are so many versions of rituals and rites. There is dark and light, healing, growing, celebration, energy raising, giving thanks, and so the list goes on.

Rituals can be great fun and energetic or musical, spiritual, self-empowering, you name it. Others can be long and tiring, solemn, serious and draining. You may also come across really boring and uninspiring rituals. Actually, you *will* come across one of these at some stage. Like life, you get the good, bad and the boring. Think of it as a lesson for when you host your own ritual. Take the information with you, what to do and what not to do for your own rites, but this will only be after you have experience and knowledge. Do not practice on friends just to show off, particularly ones that you don't really know and especially those who are not pagan as they won't have a clue — *look at me I'm a witch*!

You are dealing with other people and need the experience and knowledge of what to do if someone freaks out! You could be looking at not just physical but psychological fallout. Are you up to that as well as a possible court case? Yes, there are legal issues that can affect you if you screw up. Pretty much all rituals that include the public have insurance, and the hosts may have done a training session through one of the organizations such as PANinc (Australia) or they will have trained through a coven, group or grove, or generally be very experienced.

I've been to some interesting rituals and rites, some very thought provoking and others also scary and confronting. This is where we go back to being informed. Talk to the circle members and ask questions beforehand and afterwards ask about their personal experience.

The story I tell you further down changed lives, not all in a good way. Several years ago I went to a rather interesting full moon ritual that was funny, but started on a whole different level. I also had only known the people for a short time. They were very text book shall we say. Now remember that energy comes in all different forms, one of these is laughter (a great energy source) but there is also harvesting your own energy through chant or dance for example. Actually I believe you should use all the senses, and remember what you give to the universe you also get back and this is vice versa as well.

As a first timer going to a ritual, you are understandably a bit nervous or apprehensive, and it might be an idea to go to a public full moon circle and just observe and then later talk to the organizer/s about what you saw and felt.

On some occasions the group has what is called a *guardian*, basically that's witchy-poo talk for a person that hangs outside the circle to do a bit of public relations such as talk to passersby if they stop to watch. The guardian will talk and explain events to the people watching that are interested but not ready yet to join in and also to deflect any possible trouble without the circle being disrupted. The taking of photos is a no-no (passersby tend to do this), as are cell phones going off during the rite. Both will get you a glares and reprimands as will disruptive behavior such as whispering to your friend in the circle or during the ritual.

Usually the person running the ritual will introduce themselves and give basic rules like reminding everyone to turn off phones. They will then give a bit of an overview of what will happen, so pay attention! Listening is a good thing as sometimes you might have to pass on a short sentence to the next person. Mistakes get made not just from the newbies but even the regulars and yes even the priest and/or priestess (shock horror), so don't worry there are several outcomes to this, apologetically grin and get on with it and start again with fingers crossed or total chaotic laughter, or start again and *listen* and *hear* to what the instructions are. If the priest or priestess make a mistake they are usually pretty good at covering it up unless it's a major brain blank, then it gets interesting. This is all part of, *don't take yourself too seriously*, grins, sniggers and laughter are all part of the joy of it all. Of course if it is a full on (purpose) ritual it would have been well rehearsed so even a little mistake will be covered without most of the group even realizing, and the atmosphere will be somber if that was the intent of the rite and you will be in that mind frame. The energetic happy flamboyant rituals will have you bouncing around trying to contain all the bubbly energy feelings.

My dog just reminded me, literally another mistake not to make is farting, particularly the silent deadly kind (smelly, dead fish type) especially during a meditation or serious part of the ritual. So watch what you eat before you go, stay away from the likes of baked beans, cabbage and curry, and goddess forbid, all of them at the same time. If you don't, it's just plain and simple intestinal suicide, for as well as knocking out the ritual members you will probably give yourself a brain hemorrhage from the force, a bit like spontaneous rectal combustion, very nasty, and those that survive will probably send you to some weapons dealer overseas.

Back to the story I was going to tell. I still giggle at the thought. At a full moon ritual, a new person just wanted to observe, of course that's fine, but the priest and priestess were very serious and rather straight-laced and had the sense of joy and humor of a beetles kneecap. This they carried in the outside realm (real-life drudge world) too, anyway *Murphy's Law* or *Chaos Theory* must have come into play. During the calling of the sprits and ancestors of the land, just as the spirits were called and welcomed to enter the circle a huge and rather decomposed explosion bombarded us followed by "Oh God!" from behind the trees. The offending bottom then turned and took flight at full speed in the dark with the priestess screaming like a banshee at him "and the Goddess don't forget the Goddess!." The priestess was mortified, and the priest looked perplexed but between the screaming and squawking of the priestess came the sounds like an echo getting further away as we heard, "Sorry, sorry, don't turn me into a slug," by this stage the group of fifteen were rolling around laughing like hyenas. We received a death stare, which cut like a knife, but it was one of those instances that the circle training took over, we went instantly silent, but holding in the giggles was too much. Then a miracle happened, the priest and priestess looked at each other and slowly a smile began to gather force then a grunt was heard then a giggle, and that's when we went really silent watching in awe, it was like a planet being born. The bum culprit changed lives that night. The ritual was changed to light-hearted fun, and what was really energizing it was an impromptu make-it-up-as-you-go-along type of thing which ended up being absolutely brilliant. Everyone enjoyed it and the priest and priestess were happier more relaxed people and enjoying life more on both sides of the circle.

Mr. Bottom is most probably still on the run, ignorant that he would have been welcomed for cakes and ale, in this case red fizzy, lemonade and homemade biscuits. But the thing is that's why the experienced people who conduct rituals are so important, the ritual went on, but on a different tack almost as if it was planned but they still had control so it didn't get out of control.

The Australian pagan community is still relatively small and bad reputations get around fairly quickly. The same might apply to smaller countries such as Ireland, or states and areas where there is a strong Christian community. I think the best thing would be contact one of the major organizations and ask them what they know. As with the general world we live in, there are some unscrupulous pagans that claim to be some big high ancestral high priest/ess, whatever they want to call themselves and who will pounce on a newbie. Use your instinct and common sense, if your guts say no, listen to them, then go away, leave at once. Also report any of this dubious activity; it is *not* the pagan way. Do not be enamored with words because if it feels wrong it will be whatever pathway it is whether it is witch, druid, or pagan. You will soon get to know the real people who will help you learn and grow and will protect you as you do.

The Ritual

Ritual is in our daily life, all cultures, races, age and gender. We prepare for these rituals all the time without even realizing it. If you think about it, ritual was started as soon as we entered this world and our parents organized us into some sort of routine. For example getting ready for work or bed, waking up and preparing for the day even preparing and having a meal, it's all a ritual but the word we use is "routine." On the other hand you can have ritual that is not just day by day automatic routine, a ritual specific for a certain reason and performed a certain way. There is no right or wrong way to do this, though some will disagree, particularly traditionalists, but it's an individual choice.

When doing a specific rite with other people it's a little different as there is a basic formula that needs to be considered. As with a book it needs a beginning, middle and an end. As far as creating a ritual, the beginning and end should be shorter than the middle. Whether it is for a full moon or a sabbat, it's a good idea to have a theme. The theme might be for a welcoming or farewell ritual, one to honor your deity, or simply for a gathering, in fact there could be many reasons.

When starting out keep it simple. Some folk say the whole thing should be memorized but it's your ritual so if you want to read it, then do so, especially if it is long or complex. However if you are going to do this don't use scraps of paper as it looks bad if you're in company. Buy or make a book or BOS (Book of Shadows) or at least something to disguise the scraps of paper such as a folder. Remember to keep it somewhere safe as you might need it in the future, that's why most people have a BOS. When you are looking for something to open your ritual, decide what feels right to you. A poem or rhyme might be your choice, impromptu words that just pop into your head, or words that you memorized simply because you like them. When you are writing your ritual you can have the same opening and closing that you use each time and therefore will remember them over a short period of time.

After some time you will be confident and can expand the ritual. So find an opening that suits you first. You might want to use something from a specific tradition, or take bits from different traditions that you have read about, after all if they didn't want you to use them they wouldn't have printed them. You could go completely commando and write whatever comes to you and this I think is the best option as it comes from you, your deity, your heart and spirit and will have real meaning and that is what gives it power. Think about what actions you are going to do, what tools you want to use. Opening and closing the circle can be the same but in reverse or different. Try practicing until you come up with what feels right to you.

If you use them, think about your compass directions or calling quarters. Some people follow the Northern Hemisphere here in the south. Others go opposite to the North as in Australia all the rituals I have attended go anti-clockwise and others go geographical and match to the location which makes more sense to me. It can be a little weird when you call fire and you are looking at the ocean so it makes more sense when you have your ritual space chosen look around and see what is where. For example the full moon space where I live has an open area to the east or air, the north is dry farmland and fire, west is the lake and so water, and to the south are the mountains or earth. I have been to other rituals around Sydney, Victoria, and Queensland and each one of them called the directions differently and this can get confusing. Ingrained with my own choice of directions, I messed up when fire was in the *East* and I called out *North* so we had two calls to the North which confused some newbies and no one at the ritual even realized it until it was quietly pointed out afterwards, so that was a bit of a kick in the dignity. Mistakes do get made so don't go flogging yourself over it. I am sure Deity and Quarters snigger at us mere mortal idiots it's okay to make a blunder and you will usually only make it once and learn from it. Just be careful not to mess up completely and name the moon as male then you just might see some divine intervention. There are people here in the Southern Hemisphere that follow Northern Hemisphere directions, but I just can't get a grip on it. I find it difficult to take part in an Ostara (Spring Equinox) ritual with everything around me looking dead, the sky grey and freezing cold conditions. The same goes for doing a winter solstice in midsummer. As far as I am concerned we are completely opposite to the Northern Hemisphere with even water going down the drain in the opposite direction and our sun and moon rise and fall in the opposite directions. This is something else in the already long list of decisions to think about, so just do what feels right for you. The same reasoning applies to opening and closing your ritual, calling the quarters if you do so, and walking a circle *deosil* or *widdershins*.

The Circle

The opening and closing of a ritual circle are different things to different people. For example some people will close the circle at the beginning, their thought is that the circle has been joined and everyone and energy is within, then at the end of the ritual they open the circle basically meaning that it is no longer joined, so this is confusing. Some people say the circle is *cast* then *uncast*. If you write out your ritual think about whether to share the opening and closing with others or call everything yourself. If you are using different people to call the Quarters make sure they will definitely be there or you will end up with last minute panic.

For the guts of the ritual think about the purpose of the ritual. Is it a quiet solemn event, fun, loud and energetic or noisy or is there a theme? If you have a basic ritual written out that is generic you can add bits to suit the occasion. The middle part of the ritual is the section in which everyone in the circle can take part. You will need to keep control so everything freely flows and is timed correctly. Think about if you going to use technology such as CDs, battery operated items, or lights. I tend to use five colored lanterns (red, blue, green. yellow and white) that hold tealights. I use these particularly in the winter as it tends to warm you while your body is in spasms from arctic wind and cold. In warmer weather much of the time I have on my altar a clay dish for incense (air), an enclosed lantern with a red candle burning (fire), an abalone shell with water in it (water), and a wooden dish full of dirt (earth). I also have a Himalayan rock salt light that is lit by a battery which has a lovely look and feel, and I use for Spirit. It gives enough light to

Kimi Ravensky

see by without tearing into your retinas. Also on my altar I have a wand or athame and a chalice as well as other things I need depending on the occasion. My big secret is that I use a big box which contains all sorts of wonders and it can't be seen as it is under the altar cloth. I have everything I could possibly need in it. Yes it is a pain carting it all around but at least I know I have everything. That way if I do forget something or the flames go out, I have instant supplies and hopefully don't look like a completely forgetful idiot. I also have a written list of supplies so I can see what I need to get if stocks run low. Other than the salt light I do not used more technology than that out of doors.

Guided Visualization

If I include a visualization, I prefer to do the guiding myself or have someone else do it particularly at public rituals, then I am free to watch and make sure everyone is comfortable and they don't fall so deeply into it that they don't want to come back and keep everyone waiting for hours, even dropping off to sleep. If this happens to you just give them a bit of a gentle nudge. Some guided visualizations I find are far too long and actually prefer to do it alone. One thing about meditation and visualization is how experienced the person is, and as I've been doing both since early childhood I can go to where I want or see what I want very quickly. In a mixed group of different levels I find that if I know the visualization I am already there while others are still at the beginning.

Not so long ago I was at a workshop and experienced a taped visualization, it was awful as the CD stopped and chopped and changed and was all over the place. There was even different music and even the visualization changed. After a while I'd had enough and left while my companion stayed and endured the rest. I then promptly tried to bribe him to take me home, it put me off the whole weekend but we steeled ourselves and stayed on. So be careful with what you are doing with visualizations and perhaps have a few practice runs. Ask someone else with fresh eyes and ears to give you an opinion.

Chants

I love chants as they make you feel invigorated. Chants are great for energy raising you can also have noise makers, rattles, drums, flute, two sticks or anything you wish to accompany the chant, it's totally up to you, however, this will need control. Start off slow and work up speed and/or loudness but it's best to stop abruptly when you have hit that right moment and the gained energy is then released. If you keep going and get slower and softer it's more like a fizzle, so let everyone know when to stop either by telling them how many times you going to do it or give them a prearranged signal that you will give when it's time to stop. For those that have stood aside because of physical limitations they are then just as much a part of this and the energy is felt just as much as the participants as everyone is chanting.

If you have decided on a howl you really have to be on your toes to keep it going for the desired length of time so it might be an idea to have a signal for each time the volume is going to go rise and is another reason to explain to everyone exactly what you are doing. If you are working with the same people regularly you will all get to know instinctively and have a good rapport with each other.

These are some of my chants. I personally like to keep them short and simple basically because I can't remember long or complex words. If you write a chant that you like the beat of it's just a matter of changing the words to suit the occasion. Having a nice thumping rhythm to it makes the whole thing easy, and if you forget the words you can lip sync and sing the beat. Just hope that you all don't forget the words at the same time but then the chant is rattling somewhere in your head and the noise that is in the beat will still raise energy.

Wind, wind, spread the seeds,
May you grow for our harvest needs.

Hail, hail, the leaves are crowning,
The sun is now here, the earth is growing.

Stirring of life has now begun,
Honor be to the quickening sun.

Dark of winter, dark of night,
I see the goddess shining bright.

Hail, hail, to the longest night,
Dark now goes with the coming light.
Fare thee well to the longest night,
Short is the day but the sun is in sight.

Hail, hail, to the coming light,
Health and healing love and care,
On this earth we must share,
East, west, south and north,
Blessings all I now send forth.

Sleep, sleep, the leaves are falling,
The cold winds blow,
The winter is coming.

Circle Work

By this stage you should have an idea of you want to do and say in your ritual, here's a simple version of creating your sacred space.

Walk the circle three times round.
By thought and will the circles bound.
Guard without and guide within.
The circle's cast and can now begin.

There are so many versions of circle casting, some people use tools such as athames or wands, some nothing at all. It's the intent that counts. The goddesses and gods really don't care about the tools and paraphernalia though they are useful for channeling the energy. What is important is your belief, your commitment and to be true to heart. You can perhaps be more traditional and follow blindly, but as with us here in Australia who are relatively new but revolving at a fast rate and are making our own traditions, there is nothing wrong with making your own tradition too. If it feels right do it I am sure the Divine will let you know if it is not acceptable. So follow your instinct, heart and soul. Why memorize anything at all. Go commando and make it up as you go along, the gods and goddesses will give you guidance. If you are going to cast a circle with others present

though, do have a plan so everyone knows what is to be expected and give everyone a run down before you start. Remember to get them to turn off the cell phones, to go to the bathroom and do whatever else needs doing making sure you have everything you need so you can focus.

As I have mentioned before, I have attended many rituals of different kinds. One of the latest was hosted by Gypsie Lee (Kylie) who is well known in Sydney and is considered a dramatic ritualist. I love her rituals and she goes to amazing lengths to ensure that every sense you possess (and then some) is included. The latest one was for Beltaine and there were flowers and garlands abound, men and women of every age and background and the best thing was that the numbers of each sex were almost equal. We had spent the morning making besoms, having fun and enjoying each other's company. Food was passed around and we fumbled with the broom part, attaching it to the handle part, and wishing we had just one extra hand to hold something while it was rearranged for the third time and tied. But we did conquer the skill and our new besom was then rubbed with flying ointment. After a bit of a break and preparing the feast food and drinks, there was time to change, our clothes. I chose a green pixie outfit that had only just arrived and had a garland of flowers in my hair. I thought I could pass for a maiden, albeit an old and decrepit one, but it was the fun of it. The excitement started to build, the heat of the day was cooling and all preparations attended to. Soon it was all ready and like a gaggle of excited kids we were taken to the ritual site at the back of the backyard and there before us was a beautiful flower and wreath covered archway. The boys had a robust and very male sanded pole waiting nearby as we couldn't have our supermen getting splinters when they are off to be warriors to conquer the Yoni. I know at least two that would have squealed like fragile maidens (you know who you are!).

The ritual began with Kylie dressed in period costume

though with a modern twist that suited the occasion of the joining of time, setting the mood with verse, evocation and enchantment, her voice weaving a vision within our imagination and magical self, waving and weaving her hands around with great dramatic effect to encapsulate and punctuate each word. It didn't take long for the spirit of Beltaine to envelop the space, we were within it, it was part of us, in us, and around us.

The purpose of the ritual was to fly on our newly made and anointed besoms back to 1865 to Surrey, England and rejoin with John Brakesphere and his coven to celebrate together, past and future, Northern Hemisphere and South, with the Northern Hemisphere celebrating Samhain and we Beltaine, after all the veil is thin. We crossed the veil and mixed the sabbats in time and space as with life so is death never ending.

John Brakesphere was a nineteenth century witch that Doreen Valiente was purported to receive clairvoyant messages from on a regular basis, mainly through automatic writing.

At Southern Hemisphere Samhain earlier in the year, John and his witches were evoked to celebrate their Beltaine with us so this time we went to rejoice with them. The evocations and chanting were drawing energy, besoms were flying past, the pace grew faster, time was irrelevant and the air crackled with energy. Then it was time for the girls to go off giggling and laughing to add more beauty and enticement to the archway of Yoni, and the men went off full of manly chatter about what they were going to inscribe on their "he" pole.

I decided on a whim that I would join the men, well I was dressed as a pixie and after all and they were just a rabble of blokes of different persuasions that needed direction, so I was it! They started writing their messages; you know typical man stuff at this point so they didn't even notice me, not surprisingly! You give a bloke a phallus and he's off in his own world. So I sneaked in amongst them and as I was drawing hearts and kisses on the pole I successfully infiltrated the collective male brain and directed them to write and draw romantic symbols along with their he-man scrawling. They soon realized I was in their midst, and total confusion reigned for a brief while, but a challenging hiss and snake fingers aimed at them, and with my favorite *don't mess with me stance* leveled at each of them, they caught onto the idea and went within looking into their softer feminine side. Thanks to some proper direction a masculine, fertile, warrior — but also romantically symbolized pole — was ready to attack the archway, which was already surrounded by the women looking fierce and beautiful and determined to protect their symbolic virtue.

The girls were challenged by the men and the girls challenged back, but obviously their virtue was fairly negotiable (you know who you are), as it did not take long to break through. Reunited, the man pole was then erected, ribbons at the ready. The chanting and singing started.

What a wonderful sight watching the men and women weaving in and out singing, laughing and getting caught up with the random enjoyment and frivolity as they danced, palpable energy buzzed, the ribbons were woven. This was done I think three times so everyone got a turn. My friend Bren did all three and spent the next day "maypoled" out and exhausted from the fertility energy, if he was a she I am sure he would have made himself pregnant. After all the activity everyone was hungry and thirsty so we did as we do best and settled down to enjoy the harvest of an array of foods that each person had bought along and quenched thirsts. The ritual was discussed and everyone made merry chatting to long standing friends and forming new friendships. The laughter and chatter went on till the wee small hours, the carnage seen the next morning showed it to have been a really lively ritual after party.

Not all rituals are like this, but the outcome is the same, it's bonding of a shared experience and an experience it is, so encompass it. Another ritual I attended was at Yule. Sith who is very experienced knowledgeable of the Egyptian pantheon and has been around for a long time, was asked to perform a dark rite after the Yule festivities were ended. It was suggested that it was more for the experienced practitioners as it involved confrontation of thyself and the letting of blood. The god called on was Anubis, the ancient and powerful god of the dead who guided souls to their destination but not before he judged them. Anubis weighed the hearts of the dead and if they did not prove their faith and knowledge of the gods, or were judged to be wicked, they were fed to Ammit. So it was similar to heaven and hell. The rite was powerful quite confronting and a little scary at times. Unfortunately there were a couple of newbies that were not listening said the chant wrong and spoke during meditation, but we continued on and blocked them out. I think they were spoken to afterwards or maybe Anubis got them as I didn't see them after that.

Over time you will experience all sorts of rituals and it is fine to take with you the things that you like and make it into something that is unique to you. You will notice all the different techniques the ways the ritual is performed and the words spoken so listen and learn Now off you go and get magical, just enjoy and let your spirit soar with the Divine.

A little something else to think about, as if you don't have enough already is that at rituals many people just wear plain clothes, particularly at public rites. I have noticed that quite often the host will dress in pagan clothes or at least a cape and at most large gatherings and private rituals people will often get out of their "normal" wear and happily put on their magical gear for the entirety but definitely for the main ritual and feast. You will have read about preparing yourself pre-ritual such as ritual bathing and cleansing I think it's a nice idea to have dedicated clothes as well so the whole thing is special. Coven members will dress in their particular coven robes or skyclad (not in public) as many but not all covens or groups have their own special robes, cloaks or sashes that define them from other groups. Often the dress is identical with perhaps different colored sash or piece of jewelry to denote rank or where they belong in the coven.

4

Moots, Groups, Covens and Gatherings

Harmonia on Moots, Groups and Gatherings

A moot or group can be helpful in what you learn and how you develop individually as a pagan. If you are a solitary practitioner, this can be especially true.

Going out to meet and mix with other likeminded people will help you avoid becoming to one-track minded or feeling too alone. Through interaction and contact with others, you may learn new skills or develop new interests or improve on current ones. It can help you grow and develop as an individual. Whether we have been on our pathway for many years or have just begun, we all have something to contribute. So try not to feel intimidated if you are new to paganism. Most groups welcome new members with open arms. You will not have to do anything you do not want to and can contribute to discussions as you feel able.

How Do You Find a Moot or Group?

Moots and gatherings can be found advertised through your particular area on the internet and especially through The Witches' Voice http://www.witchvox.com/. If you haven't already joined then do so and look events and gatherings advertised in your country. Look for others in your area and email them if they have allowed it to ask if they know of any moots. You may get to hear of an event, moot or gathering through networking on forums or through Facebook, Twitter, and other forms of internet social contact.

A moot is commonly called a "Pub Moot" or "Pagan Moot" in the UK and other countries, and is generally held in a pub, bar, or hotel. People of diverse pathways come together and socialize, they swap information, or sometimes someone gives a talk on something of interest. Make sure that if you join that you regularly attend to support the group as they can quickly lose momentum without it. Don't presume that others will go so you can miss it a few times. Once in a while is fine, but do try to attend when possible. What inevitably happens without the support is that the convener or conveners turn up time after time and find no one is coming and become disheartened. These groups can be very valuable to us and it is good to support the effort that others have put in to arrange and keep them going. Many town and cities have moot gatherings so check them out.

Conveners do deserve some respect for being steadfast in their commitment. So think twice about complaining about how things are run especially if you only attend sporadically. It's not you who has to sit there month after month regardless of anyone turning up.

How Do You Start Your Own Moot?

If there is no moot in your area, but perhaps you know of one or two people who would like to attend one if there was one. Why not contact them and others through networking, saying you would like to look for a suitable venue to host a moot. Some pub, hotel, or bar managers might not take too kindly to your meeting in his or her establishment if they have strong religious views, but the majority has no problem whatever their religion. If you know of a quiet friendly bar, who you think might not object, you can always ask them, or just go and hope for the best. There is never usually a shortage of places you can ask at. To a business man/woman business is business in most cases, thank Goddess!

Advertise your moot through internet websites and social networks. If you know of someone in a coven or group, ask them to pass on the information to other members. Try to get someone to help and support you rather than do it alone, this way someone will always be there, and if you are sick or on holiday then the other person can go. To have three organizers is perhaps recommended, otherwise, you can only go with what you have. Just remember they also need to commit to turning up month after month come rain, shine, meteor strike or volcano.

We recently had our first local moot and drove through torrential rain and flooded roads to get there. As eight people managed to turn up, we considered it a success and everyone had a good time, and even more people turned up the next time. We decided as a group to try a different venue each time until we found the one that fitted us the best. Call it a very slow pub crawl. We had more than fifty pubs to get through, but luckily found the right one on the second try.

In the summer months, numbers attending the moots tend to dwindle, so the conveners have to by patient that it will eventually pick up again. If only one person turns up it is worth you sitting there. If number fail to increase then re-advertise in various places or with Pagan Federations to attract more people.

Make your own Facebook page, My Space or Yahoo group for your moot to keep people interested and informed. You can let them know through this who is going to speak if anyone and remind them of the next moot and if appropriate what subject will be up for discussion.

Through a moot you will get together with likeminded people who come together in the spirit of comradeship. We can all learn from each other whether we have been a pagan for three weeks or thirty years. Everyone has interesting views to share and sometimes talking to others can remind you of or highlight something in your own pathway that has been missing or forgotten.

Online Groups
For many witches being solitary is the favored option, and made through choice. This doesn't mean that you want to be a recluse,

shut away from the world of paganism. If you live in a remote area with not another pagan in sight, then the only option is to travel to events or gatherings and as this can mean traveling great distances it can be costly. In this case online friendships might be the only way to keep in contact with likeminded people. There are plenty of online groups. However, if you want to have a regular internet moot as you live in an isolated area, then you can start a group on one of the various search engines. Try any online social network that has a chat facility, so that you can talk to each other direct, is useful. Facebook, My space, and other social networking forums, even Skype, can be a way to get to know people and make friends. I have often made friends online and then arranged to meet those same people at gatherings.

Be wary if you are young that the people you are contacting are "real" and never arrange to meet anyone on your own.

If you have a website or forum, add a chat facility to it. Make sure you have security on the website so that people have to be approved, and fill in a security code.

They can be successful and I personally have a regular online chat which is always well turned out. There are people dropping in from the US, UK and Ireland, and even from way out in the deserts of Australia (they tune in around 6.30am). Again though you still need people to back you up in case you are sick or on holiday. You might also have to be flexible and change times and days if it becomes necessary.

Going Solo

To be or not to be solitary, that is the question. Witches generally choose to be solitary through three different reasons. The first is that for many witches there is no choice as there is not a large pagan community in their area. The second is even if there is a pagan community in the area there may not be an established coven. The third is that a person has deliberately chosen to be solitary regardless of access to a suitable coven.

In the latter case, it can be just as rewarding to go it alone, as you are free to learn at your own speed. You are also free to learn what you wish and follow whichever path suits you. The majority of witches are in this category. This does not mean that anyone with a coven background is any better than you are or more knowledgeable, only that they have different experience and knowledge.

If you call yourself an "eclectic" it can attract derision from the *holier-than-thou* brigade. These people tend to lump all eclectics in the same basket under the general heading of "flufflies." "Flufflies" or "fluffy bunnies" do exist and are not necessarily eclectic. Often they are people who just starting out have not yet found their way. Sometimes there are those who call themselves a witch then fall by the wayside after becoming bored and finding it is too much like hard work. More patience and understanding could be given to "newbies" fluffy or not. Time sorts the wheat from the chaff.

Real eclectics do not take tiny bits from every culture and cobble them together. By eclectic they might mean for instance that they use certain gods and goddess from different pantheons. This does not mean they use them all. They might have an avid interest in more than one form of divination. This doesn't mean they know a little of several, but likely they will be experienced in say dowsing, scrying and tarot. So ignore the ignorant who know nothing about how an eclectic witch may work, and grow a thick skin. This can be easily said than done especially if you've been attacked by someone who presents themselves as more knowledgeable than you, purely because they belong to a coven or particular pathway. Often your ten or twenty years of experience and study are ignored when someone is attempting to put you down.

It can be the other way around of course and it could be that a person is derided by eclectics and solitaries for being in a coven and told they do not have freedom of choice; this can often be motivated by jealousy. Those in a coven might be accused of thinking themselves superior when most people are just going about their business wondering why they are being attacked. They enjoy the comradeship of belonging to a coven and a system of working they can rely on, along with organized and professional training. This doesn't mean you won't have friends as a solitary witch, and as a hedge witch I have many friends who are in traditional Wiccan covens, eclectic, solitaries and just pagan, druid or witch.

There will always be bitchiness within witchcraft and paganism and unless you live the life of a recluse you will come across it at some point. Just remember that whether you are in a coven or not, whether you are eclectic or following a particular pathway, or even if you have studied for three years or fifteen, that everyone has something to give and we can still learn from each other.

As a solitary witch, whether eclectic or not, you will need to form a system of practice. There are indeed part-time witches who practice now and then, leave it for a year and then come back to it, and still call themselves a witch. You get the same thing within any religion or craft, but as a witch you need to grow and learn and this will not happen if you are latent.

As an example of a system, and bearing in mind that not everyone is a witch or Wiccan, perhaps begin with following the Wheel of the Year. Celebrate the festivals. Join in the odd public festival to get to know others. Celebrating the fullness of the moon means that you will have a ritual at least once a month. You can also set yourself a system of study. Learn about herbs, or nature, magic, divination, or Celtic or other mythologies. Get to know and converse with your deity regularly. Try not to learn bits and pieces of this and that, so you end up more of a *Jack of all trades*. Fully study each aspect of your intended pathway and what interests you. Try to attend workshops. You will find a good selection at public gatherings.

Kimi's Advice on Covens
A coven is an assembly of (usually) thirteen witches. A coven can also translate as convent, a community of women bound by vows/beliefs and common interest. From the dictionary and Wikipedia "community" is a group of people living in the same locality, people sharing common interests, or a distinct segment

of society. Additionally, medieval script defines the words "coven," "convent" and "community," as one and the same.

Personally, I believe a coven and a community are essentially the same thing. This I will try to explain. A coven is made up of people who teach and learn, who hold a shared commitment, similar beliefs, and look out for each other. Coven comrades do and say that which will benefit all by following a code of conduct including loyalty, mutual respect and trust, and most significantly, a mindfulness of the protection of the group's survival (so to speak), or degradation, is important.

I believe similar principles apply to communities, only on a larger scale. Pagan gatherings show that over a short period time people redevelop old friendships and create new ones. A gathering can be classified as a community, even a temporary coven in some cases, untraditional of course, but the same principles do apply. Everyone at the gathering has at least one basic thread in common that bonds each and every person, even if they have differing beliefs.

There are a few things that covens offer which communities don't. The first is an energetic link between the members, a "group mind" which is the result of weaving magic as united individuals. Covens offer spiritual experiences which simply cannot occur in the same way with the solitary practitioner, although they are definitely not less valid.

Walking a spiritual path as one single unit binds the individuals together magically. This is why coven comrades can often read each other's emotions. In a coven there are fewer barriers than in a community because members have developed a closeness unmatched to the outside. Accordingly, it is easy to argue that covens and communities are completely different, but ask yourself, is a coven not a community bound by common interests? Are they not a small segment of a larger society? Luckily, as pagans, we recognize that we are all walking the same path, though on our own individual journey. The reason both covens and communities exist are for similar reasons — survival, and most notably for the recognition of the individuals within a group. Whether they are leaders or followers, the attendant's beliefs and standards and their social survival depends on it.

Other words that come to mind are *tribe, clan, organization,* and countless others. These words are commonly used and understood by the world in general and paganism alike. *Coven* still has connotations that have lasted hundreds of years, to the ignorant and arrogant. However, all these terms remain in principal one and the same thing. Indeed if anything, it is only another's perception that changes. We have as pagans in our various English speaking countries, our own identity, culture, society, lifestyle, individuality, and some could even argue — language. People from other countries come into our own countries, bringing their own culture with them, and this is accepted. Paganism should be viewed the same. In the so-called Burning Times, not only witches were persecuted, but anyone different too. Records from these times show how past covens and communities or just communities in general were fractured, making them weak and easy to dispel or overrun. Today there are several organizations that do wonderful work to prevent this, and each and every one of them should be honored for that, but sometimes sadly, fighting, politics, personal issues and ego's unravel all the work they strive to do.

When you lose the purpose of coven or community, the betterment of all as a whole, is lost too. When you lose that light because of politics, infighting and all the other aggravations, the universe goes into chaos and helps no-one. There's a saying "united we stand, divided we fall," wouldn't it be nice if our communities became a coven or community as a whole, and join all the sparks, the glowing embers, the kindling sticks and small fires that are *us*. We should unite as one big raging fire and show the universe a glowing, magical and powerful, energetic balefire or a magnificent snow flake. It doesn't matter; we are souls seeking the same thing, and the same end. We are coven and community.

To Coven or Not to Coven?

There are reasons why you should and reasons why you shouldn't join a coven. Once again be careful what you get yourself into and go and meet the future coven (if they are unknown to you with instinct on full alert). There are some unscrupulous people about or those with strange habits. A young friend of mine told me of her experience when she was invited to join a coven locally. After a bit of general chit chat to find out what level of knowledge she had and what was expected from both sides she was then informed that she was accepted and that she would be initiated at next full moon. She was expected to have sex with each and every member of the coven both male and female. Luckily she is not naive and was not blinded by their promises.

Unfortunately many young people particularly teenagers (but this is not always the case either as I know highly intelligent older people with stars in their eyes) should not even look at joining a coven until they have some life experience behind them. I don't wish to insult the teenagers or even the "twenty somethings" but as in real life there is the good bad and ugly as well as downright criminal. Do not be pulled in, with even the slightest "uncomfortable" feeling make your farewells and leave.

In general finding a Coven is not easy they do not advertize in the local paper. As you spend time in the community and get to know people and hear all the gossip of who's who (without your own input), you will work out who you feel comfortable with and the word by mouth thing works really well. Still investigate a coven even with good recommendations and discover the profile and set of rules of behavior and what you in turn will gain. There are many reasons to join a coven or group and after all the reading you have done (or should have done) you will know those reasons well by now. Really we are a pack orientated species and want to be with, learn from, input, work together, be together, form bonds and so forth but just be on your guard.

Actually the same goes for courses particularly involving much expense and a reasonably unknown person and, not always but often, claiming a title or education or even promises. I have seen this myself and then it all disappeared along with the money and promises. The people attending the course were not young and naive but intelligent people from all walks of life that somehow got caught up in the mindset that this so called high priestess had put upon them, only to be let down. Some attendees saw through it early on and walked out, but others stayed. So this is really a serious "look into it" issue and to ask yourself why you want to join. Remember the coven or group is not there for you as your personal problem solver or sounding board, so do the work that is expected from the convener of the group and do not sign any legal documents that ask for personal and financial information. Do not hand out a stack of cash; check out the person/s running the course, coven or group. It really is important to check out someone's credentials if they actually claim to be *someone*. Investigate what sort of motivation is behind them, go through your own head what would motivate you. Small donations put in the pot to help pay for candles, charcoal, incense and such, is a well-known and accepted practice, though you do get people who won't contribute.

Covens are for teaching and learning and if you are not learning then move on elsewhere and ditto if you are spending heaps of time and money on trying to recruit new members or fundraising.

As you know covens don't advertise so if you see a big sparkly advertisement claiming all sorts of things with perhaps a discounted joining fee, I would be questioning motives and asking how much else you will be expected to fork out for.

Not all covens are bad in fact most are good. I know several covens that cannot be faulted in anyway and have actually gone out their way to help a member and even the community at large. As you settle into the pagan community and use your listening skills you will learn who is good and who to avoid but the decision is yours and you will ultimately have to deal with that decision. Live your life as you feel is honest to you and honest to those that you know.

More on Covens and Groups with Harmonia

You could form your own coven if you do not really want to go it alone but have to as there is no choice. This would be an untraditional coven if you are not personally coven trained to third degree. This may possibly cause problems with Traditional Wiccans, in as much that if you are not from a established coven whose roots can be traced back to an original Alexandrian or Gardnerian coven, then it is not a true coven and any initiations gained thereof will not be recognized.

However, it could be that you form a coven that does not have a system of initiation and is neither Alexandrian nor Gardnerian and these do exist. Additionally, no false claims should be made as to the origin of the coven or the background of its leader/s. Be open and honest about your roots at all times and make it clear to anyone who joins that you have no "downlines" if that is indeed the case. A coven such as this can swap ideas and learn from each other. Make sure you have rules in place that everyone agrees with when joining which can be referred to later in cases of dispute. If any of those rules seem not to work then call a meeting and change them. Leaders will be required to keep everything in order and to vet any newcomers to ensure they are serious members. The leader/s should have several *true* years of experience (not invented).

There are two things to avoid when starting a coven or group, the *cage* and the *headless chicken*. Inexperience can cause one or the other.

The Cage

Let us just say that there is a cage and a box. Well, we have all heard of the metaphor "stepping out of the box." When we step out of the box we step out of our comfort zone. We know all the sides and area of our box and at any time can take courage to step out of it. The point here is that it is we who keep ourselves within the box and we can step out of it when we please (well, most of the time and it does mean occasionally breaking the odd rule). The box provides security and direction.

The cage is rather different than the box as the difference with it is that we are locked in. The bars are strong and rigid (no soft sides). The cage is constrictive and there is generally not as strict set of rules or regime to go with it that must not be broken. If we put a hand through the bars then the outside force field is likely to singe our fingers. We cannot just step half out or put a hand or foot through the bars to add diversity.

If you join a new group with a leader who is more of a prison warden, and you try to diversify from the set of rules your warden has laid down, you will likely come out of the group with third degree burns from all the singeing rather than third degree initiation.

If you are forming or joining a group, try to ensure it is more of a box than a cage. Question the intended leaders or leader and what their rules or policies are concerning diversity and ask can you still be an individual within the group.

The Headless Chicken

The headless chicken runs around not knowing in which direction it is headed and more often than not will collide with things or run around aimlessly in circles. If you have a group of headless chickens with no direction then it only goes to say they will constantly bump into each other. Whether or not the cage sounds confining, it is not as confining as being in a group of headless chickens.

Now let us just imagine further and say that you decide to join a group of likeminded people. There is no leader/s, just everyone pitching in. Sooner or later a group like this is likely to clash, as their wants and needs and beliefs can be so very different.

In such a group you will often get a group "know it all." She or he is the person who is the most experienced in the group and others tend to look to her/him for guidance. This is all well and good as long as that person does not really believe that they know everything. However, if you have put them on a perch they will resent being knocked off it. If someone else more knowledgeable than them joins the group then that person will be hostile towards them. Alternatively, it could be that someone else already in the group develops a talent for something or becomes knowledgeable through much study and practice and again is likely to knock the rooster off their perch. The rest of the group ever faithful to their wise rooster will chase the other person away, so all that is ever learned is from the rooster and whatever their knowledge is limited to.

In both these cases the group is in danger of lacking progression. The best way to avoid all this is not to put one or sometimes two people on a perch in the first place.

Groups do exist that meet up at pub moots once a month and this is fine, but a regular group or coven trying to form something more concrete will sooner or later have to lay down rules otherwise you get headless chickens running around, often clashing, and a lack of community spirit. I am sure that there is always an exception but to find such a group will be very difficult indeed. Hang on to it if you do and make sure you appreciate the harmony and help in keeping it that way. If you form your own group, then have a probationary period for new members and arrange workshops so that members can share their knowledge.

Pagan Organizations
You can join a Pagan Federation in your area and join in public gatherings or workshops they might arrange. Pagan Federations are in the main run by people with vast amounts of experience. There should be one in your country which may be affiliated with federations of other countries. These organizations need your support to keep going. Generally it is not costly to join. And if you take Kimi Ravensky's advice further below in *Pamper and Pagan* you could ask for membership as a gift or give as a gift to others.

5

Broom Closet and Other Issues

Kimi on Living in the Broom Closet

Now this a very real issue and does need some serious thought, as it involves not just you, but family, friends, school and workplace, but also your age and how discreet or out-there you are going to be about it. There is nothing wrong with staying behind the door whether it is to everyone in the non-pagan realm or certain people that are in your life such as family, work or school. Coming out of the broom closet is a big decision that shouldn't be taken lightly and the reactions you will get will be varied from the mundane to the extreme. Some reactions just might surprise you, as if you've told people them you are now going to worship the devil and run around naked, chucking around body parts.

I don't personally understand some of the reactions but as it's usually down to ignorance, have some informed answers ready, and remember to remind those you tell that you are still the same now as you were when they didn't know your "secret."

Age and maturity or immaturity has some influence here too, also your commitment, belief, and education on the path you have chosen. I am not trying to put down those new to the path, however coming up with educated answers will be required and if you are young you may have to face the "it's just a phase" thing. If you are just doing the young person *look at me* thing and showing off to your mates at school, along with showing them a witch book or two and yelling out "I am a witch" well you will get your own personal Salem-like trial and will be ostracized and even laughed at.

I personally had no choice on several fronts, but also chose to tell certain people by subtle means such as wearing my pagan jewelry a little more prominently. On the odd occasion I would hint at my paganism to spark interest. The most confronting outing I did was at my new workplace of only two weeks, and for which I was totally unprepared.

I was going to the Australian Wicca Conference and did not have a computer so used the one at work which was a bit naughty. I downloaded the information I required then happily went on to look at other pagan websites and all in blissful ignorance. I would say that the next day was one of my toughest. I was called to my boss's office and she had a handful of pagan photographs I had printed the night before. As if that wasn't bad enough, I had also — and I still don't know how — somehow hacked into the mainframe of my workplace. The next day when people came in and switched on their computers, instead of the lovely Catholic logo they were usually greeted with, they had a lovely pagan site inviting them to join a full moon ritual. As you will fully understand, this did not best please my Catholic bosses and I got a good verbal kicking in the backside. I was lucky I wasn't fired. One good thing that came out of the incident was I was able to educate my fellow workers. As I have been a witch and pagan for a very long time I was able to answer everything they threw at me. I was factual and answered with respect. I think this is why I kept my job. I did promise not to make it public in the workplace and this was a fair request as I worked for a Catholic company and knew this when I started there.

So be careful you don't "come out" at your place of work like I did, as you may not be so lucky. I wonder why it should be such a big issue to start with. After all the other religions don't seem to have the same stigma attached to them. I do have rights that I could have exercised but sometimes it's best to just go with the flow, and it really does depend on the particular situation. At the same time, don't forget your rights so check them out in your own country, in Australia that is PANinc, who are really solid and know their stuff. Many governments also have laws against religious discrimination, so perhaps look them up before opening the broom closet door.

So let's get on with it. Opening the door or not, some reasons to stay hidden are because you are unsure within yourself, still discovering and learning, and not sure which path you want to tread. The decision is yours and the timing belongs to you too. It's totally a personal choice so do not be pushed into it.

Some people stay in the closet because they feel that their belief is their's and their's alone and do not want to share it, as it is sacred to them. Another reason people stay in the broom closet is the very rational fear of response. Remember that if you tell one person it will likely come back to you in the form of Chinese Whispers. What started out as a whisper that you are a pagan comes back to you in the form of gossip that you are a cat slaughtering pygmy worshipper, (not that there is anything wrong with pygmies this is just an example).

School and workplace I personally think should be kept out of the picture unless you work at a liberal workplace or go to a liberal school. After all you are going there for a purpose and both places need your full attention. There is nothing wrong in keeping your school/work life separate from your home life.

If you go to a school that has a specific religious education then you don't necessarily have to opt out of the lessons on religion. Many lessons cover not just Christianity but Buddhism and other religions which are good for you to learn about. One thing pagans are not and that is discriminatory. When the time comes how are you going to debate on paganism if you don't have both sides of the story. There are interesting questions to ask when events are presented as a truth such as if Noah took the animals two by two into the ark, wouldn't this cause inbreeding? And how did Noah fetch the animals from the other continents? These are rather tame questions and I came up with some much more interesting ones and spent a lot of time standing in the corridor like a dork after a tongue lashing and being chucked out of the classroom. Not that I recommend it.

You could say that I have several *lives* that are separate from one another. I have pagan friends and non-pagan friends. My immediate family knows what's in my closet but not my wider family. Sometimes these do mingle but they just think I have "interesting" friends. I do love my totally pagan times when I can let loose and just be myself. Not that you can't be that with others, it's just that you hold a part of yourself back. But then doesn't that apply to everyone? We all hold something of ourselves back and have different personas for different people and places.

I think the main reason people want to come out of the closet is for the purpose of being freer to discuss issues, thoughts, beliefs, and to be able to wear that massive pentacle or the clothes that are kept in the cupboard and only come out at gatherings.

There is still technology to consider for instance Facebook or just your own laptop or computer. Computers are not as private as you think, nor are your Facebook or My Space pages. So be careful of accidentally outing yourself.

Perhaps you should write a pros and cons list before you make a final decision on how you are going to go about coming out of the broom closet.

Many of my friends *trickled* out. You know the tiny pentacle, the odd not too scary book lying around and the occasional witchy word. You could ask them or others some advice on how they went about it. Or ask new friends at rituals and gatherings.

There is no need to rush this. The choice is up to you and there is no right or wrong way to do it, unless of course you get yourself burnt at the stake or a ducking then perhaps that was the wrong way but at least you are out.

Remember that once you open the broom closet door it can't

be shut again, so think long and hard about it.

Blessings to whichever choice you make.

Harmonia on Pagan Pride and Prejudice

We are all proud to be pagans but many of us remain in the broom closet because of prejudice or fear of what others will think, quite often these are family members. We might drop a hint to people by mumbling about "earth based spirituality" or "New Age" or even "Nature worshipper" avoiding the word pagan or *Witch* at all cost. I have done this so I know. We also might leave clues around such as books, cauldrons, plaques of the goddess or Green Man or perhaps a besom that allow people to wittingly or unwittingly guess our interests.

I contacted a childhood friend via an internet networking website and after several emails decided to tell her my beliefs. I never heard from her again.

Ten years ago when my youngest son was nine years old he went to stay overnight with his friend of four years. The same day I dropped him off I received a phone call to come and collect him. My husband and I arrived at the house to meet the hysterical parents. Apparently my son had told them I was a witch. An argument ensued with me trying to explain I was not a Satan worshipper. In the end I gave up, telling them they had very narrow views. On the way home my son told me that they had sat him down and were grilling him and asking strange questions one of which was, "Have you ever heard your mum talk about someone called Charles Manson?" To which my son innocently replied, "No, but she likes Charles Bronson!"

Some people are afraid of reprisals against themselves, partners or children. They may be afraid that their children will be bullied or ridiculed because of their beliefs.

We each have to decide for ourselves. We should not be pressurized by the "Proud to be Pagan" gang. On the other hand sometimes it is just a case of taking the bull by the horns and

coming out. However, in every country where I have lived (I have travelled a bit), I have chosen to do this gradually, feeling my way first.

In the UK and the Netherlands I found the whole coming out of the broom closet easier as there were so many of us about. I decided once to gather a few non-Pagan friends together, most of which were spiritual people in their own ways, to celebrate Samhain. I wanted to show them that it was not all serious or indeed frightening. My idea was to cast a circle and then sit and remember our loved ones who had passed to the Summerlands, following it up with some apple games and feasting.

Not knowing what to expect, my friends all sat around and the tension was obvious, with everyone taking it all very seriously. I could not find my usual music (to relax my guests) so running late grabbed at a CD by *Clannad*. Just as the tension was strongest as I cast the circle, a dramatic tune came on called *Robin the Hooded Man*, from a UK TV series about Robin Hood. At that point it sounded so corny that it threw me off completely and I add a terrible urge to giggle. I was glad that at some points my back was turned as my grin was becoming obvious and I was praying for the song to end. My guests had not noticed at all and sat solemnly and nervously waiting for what would come next. Although nervous I knew they were actually hoping for something they had never before experienced, and I did not want to ruin it for them, so I did not tell them until the feasting (and to lighten the mood). The moral of the story is to choose music carefully when inviting non-pagan guests to your rituals. If this had been with fellow pagans I would have inanely grinned, stopped, and replaced the music or switched it off, probably to howls of laughter. We do have to treat people in different way according to who they are.

By contrast it had not been so easy to come out where I live now. People had warned me not to be so open in very Catholic Ireland and to feel my way first. So after doing the round of "I'm close to nature" and mumblings of "earth based spirituality" I was asked to do both a radio and newspaper interview. With the article, I was expecting a slim column tucked away somewhere, but my picture alone took up half a page and the interview the rest, and on the center pages. Both the word "Witch" and "Pagan" were prominently used, so that was me *outed* to many people. I have not received any prejudices or negativity to date, though an elderly lady of my acquaintance told me she had seen the article and that people were afraid of those things, but if I was to offer money charms I would have a queue from here to kingdom come! I am still careful nevertheless and tend to equivocate with terms when talking to people I do not know.

Perhaps the day will come when we can all openly wear the tee-shirt "Proud to be Pagan."

Stop it! — Advice from Kimi

We are all bound by a common thread and if this thread is unraveled it becomes weak and can be pulled apart by any wacko or over the top religious nut-job and there are plenty out there. In all walks of life there seems to be a bit of dissension as humans are human and there is occasionally trouble such as disagreements or an all out fight wars and clashes of personality. This happens not just on the one to one basis but within groups, covens and between various groups. Sometimes it is *someone* at an event who causes problems, and even parts of the community seem to go through periods of upheaval every now again where people are accused of things, gossip runs rife, and all hell breaks loose in general.

No matter what part of your country you are in, as a newbie you get snippets of gossip and told, "Don't go to that or avoid them because —" or "Go to this and show support for that —." It's up to you to decide, so go to what events *you* want to go to. Do not get mixed up in infighting so early in your discovery and journey. Sometimes when emotions are running on overdrive you may even be accused of taking sides even though you don't have a clue what's going on so better to stay out of any arguments. If you can't make up your own mind with sincerity and conviction and if you know the people concerned really well and what their true heart is, you can make an informed decision of where you want to go to. It's always best not to take sides, or should I say to try not to take sides. If you are pressured into taking sides distance yourself as no good will come of it for anyone and everyone loses. A "them and us" situation rarely works except of the destructive kind and most of the time the full story is not told, just one side of it.

The mayhem is usually down to one or two personalities clashing whether it is for their own gain or notoriety, ego, or just because of a difference of opinion or even an insult intended or not. The problem could be a political view that just gets overheated, we are complex creatures are often misunderstood and this leads to all sorts of strife. At this point when you are new to the community, group or coven, it's really a good idea to do the ostrich thing and put your head in the sand until it all blows over letting the warring parties work it out for themselves, and hopefully they will be mature enough not to involve others. It's enough we have to stand up for what we believe in, but there are ways of doing it and the little bitchy things are just a waste of energy. If you want to have a go at someone don't do it on a public forum or you will face all sorts of chaos coming straight at you. That's why the word "private" was invented so we could use it.

If you have a conflict with someone else try to sort it out together or agree to disagree, and get on with better things. Sometimes just walking away will make you the stronger person and if they keep going at you ignore them, you have better energy to embrace. Let their universal law deal with them. One thing we all need to remember is that we are not in danger of being burned at the stake after an ignorant and misinformed torture and trial that ultimately ends in physical death, but we are in danger of the same thing only on a psychological level. If you have a problem with someone, go and talk to them or someone of trust for advice but keep opinions to yourself. A secret shared is not a secret. If you share something you don't want known, you have a cat's chance in hell that it will remain so. The odds are on that it will be passed on to another *trusted* friend and in doing so opinions and thoughts are unwittingly passed on and the story changes and I can guarantee your name will be there however the story ends up. It's like playing a game of Russian roulette!

Sometimes someone comes up with an idea or plan and gets shot down by someone who says it can't be done because of this and that and then they come up with hurdles. In this case it's best to find a way over those hurdles and get on with it or ask the hurdle maker their suggestions (after all they came up with them). If you are the hurdle maker unless you have organized something you have no right to witch-bitch and you should be constructive not destructive. Work toward to common good of the community and forget your own ego. I am sure you will get all the praise and whatever else you searching for at some stage so there is no need to put others down or witch-bitch so you can feel good about yourself. Just because you are pagan whatever path it may be gives no one the right to use it for unscrupulous behavior. But unfortunately like the non-pagan realm, we do have some sleazy people who claim all sorts of things and are like spiders with a web to trap the naïve, so please be cautious.

Hint

I have found that those that brag and rave of *who* they are, usually are not anything important. They feel the need to be "someone special" and are really saying "look at me!" The ones that say nothing but have that *something* about them, they are the ones you should go and talk to, because they don't need the ego boost.

Never Ever Issues!
- Never ever distrust your first gut feeling!

- Never ever disregard the legal requirements when at a

public ritual, such as what can be classified as weapons, alcohol, nudity, or whatever!

- Never ever step in after ritual has begun and do *your thing*. It's not your ritual dipstick.

- Never ever be disrespectful of your host/s because you have another view.

- Never ever disdain people that do not join in rituals but stay on the sidelines as there are many different reasons for this.

- Never ever join a coven or group if you are asked to do something that you don't really want to.

So all that said I once again have a story to tell you. I was on a hill in another state for a ritual a while ago and I decided to watch instead of participating. The circle was cast and the participants were told their roles and all was perfectly arranged by the host who is a very experienced witch and a lovely lady. She was about to start her "in circle" workings when someone stepped in and started doing their own thing. The members of circle wondered what was going on but in her magnificent style the host gave them the nod. Others though were quite upset with this new to ritual person screwing it up, and not knowing what the person was going to say or do. They knew the site's history and that it had blessings and it belonged to them. I was informed it was formerly a refuse dump and was covered over and turned into a park surrounded by every modern day convenience you could think of and see. However, a bit of green in the middle of urban chaos is still bit of green Anyway, the silly person was lucky they were not pulled down by wrath impersonate, but the circle gave respect and time to this person that was not given to them, and then continued as planned.

The next *never ever* of the night was another young idiot asking for a corkscrew. That person was told rules apply not only for circle but also for the countries laws of public drinking. The thing is that the organizers bear responsibility for what is done on site so just follow basic rules and laws and have some respect for them. This is basic respect 101.

6

Rites of Passage with Kimi

Some of the ways that we celebrate our life and mark special events such as birthdays, anniversaries, weddings, births and funerals, are common in all walks of life, cultures and religions, not just the world of witches or pagans. Often these milestones are celebrated and viewed differently, for example some cultures do not speak about birth, and death is viewed as taboo. Puberty in nearly all cultures is something that everyone squirms about and waits for it all to go away as if it's a big secret and not to be discussed. Pagans in general are quite open about all aspects of life's journeys discoveries and milestones, and of course it's any excuse for a good party or get together to celebrate and acknowledge the person who has reached a certain landmark in their life.

There is some controversy as to who should lead a particular rite, ritual or ceremony. In Australia, looking at legalities, a pagan civil celebrant (of whom there are not many) can perform a ceremony which will be legally binding as far as our legal system goes. On the other hand, elders, coven leaders, even a friend that has knowledge and experience are preferred. For some it is only an initiated third degree priest/ess that is acceptable though this is in a spiritual way only and not legal unless they are also a registered celebrant. This is the general position in many countries, and where there is no pagan celebrant available or there are no legal pagan celebrants at all, often a couple will choose to have a civil ceremony and follow it up later with the spiritual ceremony (Harmonia did this in the UK). I also have it on good authority from Harmonia that Ireland now has its own legal pagan celebrant and there are also other pagans in training in various counties owing to the very hard work of Pagan Federation Ireland coordinator, Ray Sweeney.

Basically there are no rights or wrongs about rites of passage so do what suits you.

There are several rites of passage that occur while we are in this realm and your friends, guardians and family will surely have a good time at them. Even from your birth you will have provided an excuse for everyone to get together and become a joined community even if it's only for one day. The people in your life will make an extra effort to travel many kilometers or miles to bear witness to each of your milestones. The first party you will more than likely sleep through, and the last you will be off on some long awaited holiday in the Summerland resting and preparing for your next journey. The middle milestone you will be sweating it out with nervousness but will be the centre of attention for several weeks. These three phases of life are pretty simple but there are also others nonetheless important that slip in just to keep it interesting. You have probably guessed the three big steps of the journey of life, baby naming or wiccaning, handfasting and pagan funeral rite. There are often other milestones in the pagan world and those of other faiths will add or take away from these.

Milestones

Birth, Life, and Death — you can't really do much about the birth and death part in this realm, but you can certainly do lot with the middle part of life. No matter how long or short it may be, the decision of how you live it is completely up to you and is yours and yours alone, good or bad. You are responsible for this part, no one else and you could succumb to so-called peer pressure from the bad crowd you are hanging with and screw it up or just be reckless and irresponsible, but it's still you that makes the ultimate decision and it's going to be you that will weather the consequences. If you make a bad or wrong decision and you land in hot water, whether it is to do with law, family, or community you will find the cohort friends will have buggered off by now but you may still have some true blue friends that will support you and can consider yourself extremely lucky. If it gets to this point this is where you do some serious soul searching, so it's back again to words you will hear again and again, if it doesn't feel right don't do it, if it hurts you or others don't do it. So let's get on to the celebrations.

Wiccaning

Wiccaning is a form of ceremony or ritual to bless the new born or small child, it is sometimes called a *naming ceremony* but these two ceremonies can also be separate. This is similar to a christening and of course like the typical christening the proud parents are freaking out and hoping like hell that gorgeous baby or child will stay placid, or better still, sleep and does not throw up their last feed over mum's new velvet cloak. I can tell you that baby chuck up and velvet do not mix and the smell lasts for years. Revenge can be yours so just keep it in a nice box and present it to the darling up-chucker on their 18th or 21st birthdays, and it's highly likely they will baptize it again but that will be their problem now!

The main difference between a Christening and a wiccaning is that at a Christening, the child is welcomed into the Christian belief system of the parents and it's expected to be for life and thus the child is chained to it. With a wiccaning they are bought up in their parent's faith until they are of an age that they decide for themselves where their own path is going.

Choosing a wiccaning, blessing day or naming day can be for several different reasons, such as you are not overly religious but want to do something special for your child. These ceremonies can be conducted by a pagan friend, family member or by yourself. I did say pagan rather than witch as pagan covers many faiths and each has a different slant on it but the outcome is the same.

A Basic Wiccaning Ceremony

There is no right way or wrong way, it's an individual choice and varies depending on the practitioners and their path. A wiccaning can be performed anywhere but it is preferable, and most people do choose this, is to go outdoors to a special site or somewhere close to water.

Basic Ceremony

If you have a priest and/or priestess hosting it, but there is no reason why you can't do it yourself, an altar table will be set up with tools and items that are to be used during the ceremony and which may include candles that represent the five elements (earth, air, fire, water and spirit). A circle is often cast that envelopes all present and those not comfortable with it will be moved to an area so they can see what's going on outside the circle space. The ceremony may begin with opening the circle then all those involved will do their part. Each wiccaning is individual, but essentially the ceremony is about welcoming the child, acknowledging their name, thanking and asking the ancestors, guardians, gods and goddesses to watch over the child until it can make its own decision of where it wants to travel and what path it wants to take.

The "god/goddess" parents or sponsors will be called on to accept some responsibility in the child's growth and education. Finally the participants share cakes and wine and the circle is closed.

Usually the formalities are followed by the feasting and congratulations and exchange of gifts. An idea for a gift is just to gather items and put them in a box. Items such as pins, nappies, baby wash, blankets and so forth go down very nicely. It's amazing how much stuff you accumulate over seven months or so you build up your baby supplies.

The other gift I really like is that of the blanket, where all the women that will share in the little ones life get together to sew something special and personal on it. Making a blanket is also a good excuse to get together for a bit of a yak over tea and tasty biscuits and cake, and also to pass on some wisdom to the new mum about what to expect or some handy hints. Enjoy the discoveries with your friend who is growing a new soul or maybe an old one.

Coming of Age

Now is a time when we have journeyed, grown and learnt some of life's lessons and reached a stage that we change from child to adult; the transition into another aspect of ourselves.

The celebration of puberty is for both genders but when a girl starts menstruation, she is considered a woman and many groups have a celebration for this which is usually, if not always, for women only. They gather for a ritual and party to honor the girl-woman and share their wisdom about the responsibilities she now faces with sexual maturity. As most pagan groups are very choice oriented, the girl now comes to an age when she makes her own decisions about what she does with her body. Women and elders encourage the girl to seek advice when making a big decision, such as when she feels ready to commit to a physical relationship, what contraception if any to use, and discuss issues surrounding abortion. Though Wicca in particular is a fertility religion it does not mean that everyone engages in random sex, in fact it can be quite the contrary. With the wisdom given by the elders and their own informed choice, the girl-woman makes a decision whether it is deemed right or wrong by others, taking responsibility for the outcome and consequences as is done with all aspects of her life.

With the transition of boyhood to sexual maturity less defined, it can be at the time of the boys first wet dream or the physical emergence of secondary masculine attributes such as pubic hair growth and deepening of the voice. This celebration is usually always a purely male celebration and as with the girls the elders impart wisdom but the decision of his sexuality belongs ultimately to boy-man whether he lives as gay, straight, bi-sexual, celibate and so forth.

The girls and boys that have transitioned should follow the Wiccan Rede of harm none or another similar ethic. Pedophilia and child porn, rape, sexual inappropriateness and so on are not tolerated and will be dealt with quickly and reported to the appropriate authorities.

Family

Most pagans consider family to be more than just their blood relatives but it is extended to their group, coven and friends. Similar to the average family, if you do not get on with someone you will still come to their defense or aide if they need you. Rites of passage define Wiccans, witches and pagans, and the *family* is much more diverse than many people — especially non-pagans — understand or realize.

Initiations and Dedications

Something I must start with is the controversy that surrounds initiations and it seems to be either black or white, can or cannot. Many people, especially traditional Wiccans, believe that you can only be deemed a true witch if you are either bred into it or studied with a coven and worked your way up to be initiated by the high Priest/ess, yet many others disagree and that self-dedication is just as real.

Initiation is an important rite of passage as it shows the wisdom and learning achieved. I equate this with 18th or 21st birthdays, which are recognized by pretty much every country and culture though not all. For sure westernized populations accept these ages as legally gaining adulthood, gaining the vote, perhaps a bank account or a credit card. You don't have to ask mum or dad if you can go out. You can also legally drink alcohol if you wish, but be careful as mum and/or dad can still get stuck into you when you get up in the morning looking like something that belongs in a coffin. Having reached the age of adult you have to take responsibility for your actions legal or otherwise. And so it is the same with self-dedication. You can dedicate yourself to the goddess and god of your choosing and this will be a personal and solitary ceremony.

With initiation you can be initiated at any age and it is also a personal and fulfilling time. The choice is personal when you commit to a belief system whatever that may be. The ceremony is usually presided over by either one or both priest/ess of the group or coven, grove, or church. You can also have more than one initiation because as you learn you can climb the ranks so to speak, though this is usually in the more traditional groups that have set learning goals to achieve to pass to next level. For example as an acolyte, neophyte or witch, over time and with much education you will eventually be classed as high priest or high priestess. At this point you may well choose to hive off to elder a different group or coven. Each coven and group will have their own style of initiation and different titles to give.

Handfasting

The bonding of two individuals, male-female, female-female, male-male they are bound together for as long as love may last. This does not make it frivolous where a couple can just break up on a whim or after a fight as it is expected that the couple work through their differences just as a traditional married couple would. A handfasting is not taken lightly and is much thought out by the couple as to what each expects. It's the same as any couple getting wed, it's probably a good idea to seek advice from an impartial elder as the couple can discuss their hopes, fears, aspirations and what each expects from the other. Later if there is a bit of a rocky patch, the elder can give council without taking sides, so as long as love shall last is sensible. I personally couldn't think of anything worse than sharing a life with someone after the love has gone but we all know that with traditional weddings, before writing own vows and pre-nuptial agreements became popular, people vowed to be together in sickness and in health, richer or poorer, honor and obey till death do they part. In many instances that was just asking for trouble as one of the couple had to die so the other could get out of the vows, and the

question was which one and how would they do it!

These days there are fewer people making any form of bonding for a lifetime. Most people just live together and as this is recognized by particular governments and legal rights are the same as married people.

You can be handfasted several ways, by yourselves or by

yourselves in front of friends and family, by the high priest/ess of your coven or by another pagan friend. You can also be handfasted by a legal celebrant in countries where legal pagan marriages are allowed, such as in Ireland. There are civil marriage celebrant courses in some countries that pagans are now embarking on, this is government recognized and once you have the certificate and have registered with the appropriate government body you are authorized to marry anyone either non-pagan or pagan and in this way it is a legally recognized handfasting. Some countries do not allow any religious ceremony in civil marriages and as paganism is a religion it's as well to check before doing a celebrant course in your country. If you undergo a religious celebrant course, all ceremonies will be limited to pagan handfastings only.

With the same criteria as a traditional wedding only done pagan style, a handfasting is just as lovely and more personalized than a traditional wedding and just as crazy when planning, if not more so. You will still have to take into account who is going to attend and whether that will be pagans or non-pagan, family or friends.

You will need to decide on whether or not to have a circle and who will join in, how big or small the celebration will be, fancy or themed, and where and when it will be. Just like a traditional wedding, a lot of planning and preparation is put into a handfasting as well as the usual stress and frustration. A wedding and handfasting are basically the same just called different by a different name. I personally find a handfasting much more fun and interesting than a traditional wedding. There's something very earthy and magical about it but is still fun and unless you are part of the formalities you can sit back and enjoy the glory of your friends being joined as a couple. If you are a part of the celebration you may be getting up at some ungodly hour in the cold to cut fruit or pack food in containers, remember lines, (which in my case I had down pat until I had to say them at the ceremony), get dressed and last minute dash and so forth.

Handparting

A handparting is the opposite of the handfasting and means the love ran out, at least on one side. A handfasting is often for a year and a day, or more commonly "as long as love may last" but if it's all sadly gone wrong you can have a *handparting* ceremony just to make it official and let everyone know that you are no longer together, though it's not obligatory and often within certain traditions.

A handparting can be another reason to get to eat and make merry while commiserating the split of the couple as like any split it is difficult all round with problems such as which of the couple will get custody of the appliances, animals, kids or friends. My advice would be to stay out of decisions and remember there are two people involved and two different reasons for the parting and it is for them alone to work out without interference or witchin' and bitchin' from outside. Be supportive but also neutral and let the parting take its own course.

Croning, Saging or Eldering

For us all comes the time of life where you are basically on the old end of the stick and are *supposed* to be wise and learned. Unlike general western society where old people are often ditched, the general pagan community honors them and it is believed that those who have been in the craft for twenty years or so are considered an elder and one who has wisdom. With their life experience and knowledge they have many a tale to tell and some good advice to impart. Elders may well also get the best log around the fire pit in a sense this is another rite for passing to another level of one's life.

Croning is an all girl thing and happens at menopause and

there are different ceremonies depending on belief systems. For men it's the same and I have heard that a ceremony of same sex people have a full on ritual to say farewell to the youngster and welcome the elder and to the autumn time of the wheel.

With all ceremonies, there is revelry with feasting and all that goes along with it, the only difference now is that if this person wants your bit of the log to sit on, you have to get off. You could also get them a drink or a snack or a soft cushion, logs are hard on old bottoms (wink).

Passing

Well this is it, you have passed to the Summerlands but have you made your burial wishes known. The legal requirements are different in each country or state as far as body removal goes, but services can be individually tailored to the person and it's a good idea to let whoever will be arranging the whole thing know what your wishes are. Remember that funerals are for the living, so if you are in the closet to your family you might not get the funeral they would like, but perhaps your pagan family could have a memorial for you. If you think about it, an idea would be to have a plan A and a plan B but let your pagan friends know what you want. Have a will ready also for non-pagan family and friends and you could write a message to them and let them know your beliefs. It might not change their funeral plans for you but at least they know.

I haven't been to a pagan funeral rite but knowing my luck I will be the one that gets practiced on, but that's all right cause if it's awful I will get them in the future after a bit of haunting in this lifetime.

If you know you are going to kick the bucket, it is acceptable and has actually has been around for long time in many countries, to have a living wake. This is such a good idea, as you get to hear all sorts of stuff about yourself, have a raving good time with friends and everyone can get drunk. On a more serious level (that's funny coming from me) if you are stricken by an illness or know that you are going to the Summerlands there are rites and rituals that can help you make the journey easier.

I have spoken to several people about this subject (even though they thought me weird) and I found it was a fifty-fifty choice for cremation or burial. I personally don't like the idea of rotting in some box as I would rather it was still a tree. My plan is to get an eco cardboard coffin, go and be barbecued then have my ashes put in a box. If someone wants to, they can take a bit and plant me with a tree or something, but some of me will have to go to the ocean.

I don't know why this subject is difficult for some people but it is part of our lives and the wheel is not an ending it's a beginning and all life should be celebrated, not mourned. Yes we will miss our special person but we have memories that were given to us so we can relive special moments as often as we want.

Back to the beginning and the wheel turns.

Harmonia on Handfasting Ceremonies

A handfasting in present day time is a pagan wedding (though in the old days it was for everyone), originating from times past when it was not necessary to have an officiator but couples could be handfasted by mutual consent. In modern times, in this gender neutral ceremony, it is usual for the couple's hands to be bound together with cord or ribbon.

Your own ceremony can be for all of eternity (this life and the next), for this lifetime only, for as long as the love may last, or of a shorter duration usually a year and a day, after which the couple can be handparted or renew their vows. The handfasting ceremony should not be entered into on a whim but should be considered as deeply binding as any legal wedding. And if you are lucky in your particular country it could well be legal too.

The Ceremony

A handfasting is an important event in your life and therefore should be planned according to your own wishes.

Plan, plan, plan, beforehand to ensure you have agreed the ceremony with the officiator. Decide about handfasting cord or ribbon colors, whether or not to jump the besom (although I can assure you this is fun), have a list of things that you will need and who is bringing what. Ask permissions if any. If you are having a separate legal wedding have this first and time it accordingly.

Decide in advance if there will be a circle cast. If many people are attending and a large circle is not feasible, cast a smaller circle and decide who will be in it. Everyone else will stay on the outside and children can run around without the risk of disturbing you (but have your scourge ready just in case). If you decide not to cast a circle then an alternative is to gather people around, holding hands if you wish. Perhaps you may wish to devise your own ritual for this.

With non-Pagan friends and family, let them know that they should not feel obliged to attend. Inform them of the likely content of the ceremony to save any surprised comments or reactions.

You can write the ceremony yourselves, or ask around for one, which you can then adapt. If the weather is likely to be inclement or rather hot then provide some shelter in the form of a marquee or the shade of trees, or even switch to the cooler evening.

You might want to have a more traditional reception or something as lavish as a masquerade ball. You might like a themed wedding with medieval clothing or a reenactment of some sort. Other suggestions can be a picnic, or even just drinks and cake on site and a gathering at the local pub or bar. A handfasting does not have to be expensive.

The length of the ceremony should be considered according

to the time of year. If you have chosen mid-summer think of your guests standing in the full heat of the sun. A spring, autumn or evening wedding is an alternative. My own handfasting officiator baked in her wool cloak in twenty-five degrees centigrade and was just a puddle and a witch's hat by the end. While as an officiator I froze in my velvet cloak on a mid-winter day of minus eight degrees centigrade. So planning what you wear to suit weather might be prudent.

Whether or not you have an officiator is up to you. Any pagan can do this service as long as they know the meaning of the ceremony. Find someone experienced if you wish or choose a close friend. You can even handfast yourselves. The officiator can have an assistant to prompt them should they forget the words, or use a collapsible music stand on which they can place a copy of the ceremony (placed in a nice folder or BOS) to refer to if necessary or lay it on the altar. Do not panic about mistakes, as most people will not know if something has been missed out and the show must go on.

Cords or ribbons can be used to bind the couple's hands together. Your pathway or tradition may determine the color, amount, and length, otherwise choose colors according to the symbolism. Some couples use three or more cords, some two and some only one, the length of which will also vary but is usually in multiples of three feet, with nine feet perhaps being the most popular length. Some couples weave their own chosen colors. Which hands to tie can also be decided beforehand to save confusion. You might prefer left hands to be tied, or the right, or the bride's left with the groom's right or vice versa, or even both hands of each person with the couple facing each other.

Exchanging flowers adds romance to the ceremony. Flowers have symbolic meaning so think carefully before choosing. My husband and I chose red and white roses for love and unity. You can also exchange rings.

The jollities can begin with jumping the besom to seal the

union, for general luck and to leap into your new life together as one, or for fertility. You can state why you are jumping the besom beforehand. The besom can be laid on the ground or held by two people a few inches above the ground; though if you are withering you may just want it on the ground to avoid aching hips. The couple can share in consecrated mead and handfasting cake and then everyone else can be invited to join in.

Location

The location of the ceremony need only be important to the couple about to be handfasted. A sacred site is not always possible or suitable for the ceremony. For my husband and me, outside in nature in a river setting with many trees was the most important consideration. Our own chosen site was across the road from an inn. We had the civil wedding first then moved onto the handfasting location. The inn was able to provide us and our guests with the accommodation and wedding reception.

Conveniently the inn people owned the piece of land in front of the river across the road. They kindly provided us with a table to use as the altar. The location was beautiful with many trees, and swans and geese swimming on the clear river. The day was glorious, warm, and on a full moon.

We chose our day and gave out a general invitation to family and friends with a note to say that they should not feel obliged to come, but should want to. It was more important that our own children and close friends attended. The atmosphere was relaxed. Our officiator and her assistant cast a small circle, marked off at the directional points with garden torches, and with only us and one child of each of us within it. As it happened the event turned out very well. Those who did decide to attend — both pagan and non-Pagan — commented that it was the most romantic wedding they had ever attended.

Yes things did go wrong. It is not always a good idea to iron your wedding dress last minute. It was the hotel iron I used and

I turned it to the lowest setting. It was only when the iron touched the back of the bodice and brought away a piece of material that I realized the little dot that indicates the hottest setting was at the bottom not at the top and I had turned it right up. I decided what was done was done and I convinced myself while holding in the tears it was not too bad and it would be covered by my stole anyway. I was so late getting ready that I really did not have the time to cry about it. No one said a word about it until we were in the garden after the handfasting and a woman pronounced rather loudly, "Oh Goddess, your dress! It has a hole in it!" Everyone turned around and glared at her. They already knew of course and were being tactful not mentioning it. She followed it up with a helpful, "You could have borrowed *my* dress and then you would have been as beautiful as me!" Speechless!

In contrast I officiated at a handfasting on a freezing day at Avebury Stone Circle also in Wiltshire, UK, with only a handful of people attending. It was eight degrees Celsius below with a bitter wind, too much for my middle-aged skin! We set up in the middle of a field within the standing stones, and used a collapsible table for the altar. The ceremony I realized rather too late was too long for such a cold day, not that anyone complained but their blue skin tone was a bit telling. When one guy's face turned to shades of blue and purple which did worry me a bit, I speeded the whole thing up and we went through it in fast motion. Everyone grabbed at the mead which did help a bit and then we cleared everything into the car in record time and dashed to the Red Lion for whiskey and wine. The couple I am glad to say, were just as happy with their simple handfasting as we were with ours as it was the binding together which was most important.

In choosing a location, pick somewhere that strikes a chord within you as a couple, ensuring you have any necessary permission. The location can be at a sacred site, on the beach, hillside, riverside, wood or forest, or somewhere as simple as a garden, even indoors perhaps in a hall, as long as you the couple love it.

Above all else this is a special day for any couple. If their own wishes are respected, and a relaxed attitude is taken, all will be well.

Handparting Short and Sweet

On the ceremony I have only one short piece of advice from someone in the know who kindly passed on this advice, and who just happens to be Ireland's first legal Pagan Solemnizer, Ray Sweeney — *keep it very short and choose your words carefully.*

I would totally agree with this as some witches have rather sharp nails (so protection may be needed), but in general it is advisable to keep your hands at a reasonable distance from the couple for healthy and safety reasons.

7

Let's Get Into Some Fun Stuff with Kimi

Hunter-Gathering

I love the hunter-gatherer aspect of paganism, especially when you are with other pagans or witchy friends. But be warned, competition can get quite fierce especially if you all pounce on the same object at the same time, then it's each witch for themselves, and the survivor gets the trophy but also has to fork out for the coffee and cake to the vanquished.

Do not openly gloat in front of them as they could turn on you like a dingo having a bad day with a migraine after a bout of diarrhea, so wait until you are safe at home then you can gloat all you want and experience those emotions that Gollum from *Lord of the Rings* felt each time he was with his "precious."

There are four distinct categories in *hunter-gathering*:

- Lots of Dollars
- On the cheap
- Freebees
- Road kill

Some people like the **Lots of Dollars** category. They see the list of tools, accessories, clothes and so forth that are "required" and go around shopping at all sorts of places like galleries, antique dealers, websites filled with exotic handmade swords, expertly carved wands that look just like you picked it up off the ground and other highly polished or jewel encrusted items, eBay limited edition stuff, or one of the pagan shop websites that sell mass produced but sometimes special item made by High Priestess Whatsit and blessed by the spirit of Gerald Gardner.

This realm you really don't need, or have to go into huge debt for just because you think it's best to have the most expensive wand or chalice. Yes people will admire it, but really they don't care how much of your soul you sold to acquire it.

Did you know that it is an historical fact that there weren't any of these places around in the ancient or old days of the Craft? Shock horror they didn't have eBay! So where did they get their magical tools? From the gifts the bosses created for us, the earth, flora, fauna, rivers, oceans, own imagination, creativity, skill and so on. Why do some feel the need to have shiny or a perfectly made athame or lathed bowl, the ermine lined antique rich velvet cloak/dress, and jewelry that costs the same to feed a small third world country. The goddesses and gods don't care, but at least they know you had fun getting ripped off.

The second **On the Cheap** category can be quite an adventure, especially with a mate or two and it's amazing the different interpretations that you get. What to you is a shabby old cup is a future chalice to the creative thinker, the broken and forlorn little side table that can be transformed into a fabulous altar with a bit of imagination and some hands on craft skill.

A friend of mine has the most wonderful altar cloth made from exquisite fabric that looks like it came from an emperor's palace, but in fact it is the cut up skirt of the ugliest dress I have ever seen, with an added bit of embroidery and some cheap but pretty bling tastefully decorated and *voila*! An altar cloth worthy of absolute envy, greed, and lust. Want, want, want, and a new spark within you that has you roaming the shops and secondhand places looking at ugly clothes, while the shopkeeper looks at you wondering if you were born with bad taste or you have some sort of brain injury. He might also be pondering whether he should tell you that if you wear that hideous, not even your size, concoction you will be committing fashion suicide. I have found shopkeepers are a bit curious and often ask, "fancy dress party?" as this is their way of trying to save you from fashion embarrassment, so just explain it's the fabric you are after. A few times I have been shown some "too ugly to put out front in the shop" clothes, but the fabric was fabulous.

When doing the hunter-gathering at the shops, secondhand places, even markets or garage sales, the local tip, and don't forget the dumpster that you happen to come across and have a quick snoop over, there are a lot of hidden treasures to find. Of course sometimes you get lucky and come across something that is exactly what you want and all it needs is a clean up or polish. These rare items are what you fight over when you are with friends. So remember to take extra money for the coffee and cake and by doing this it's a re-affirmation that you will be the victor not the vanquished. It gives you all something to talk about and swap ideas with, while enjoying the after-hunt feast of drink and food and watching peoples facial reactions as they go by your table looking at the pile of rubbish in the centre and wondering why you all look so happy, (remember non-pagans have no idea but we know why). Another reason to go with other people is that they can come up with ideas you might not think of to transform some obscure object into a piece of beautiful and much loved *objets d'art*, altar, working magical tool, and so on.

Yes now what you have been waiting for, the **Freebees** category — the off the ground, out of the bin, from the tree, and even road-kill (not for the faint-hearted) this is a minefield of great stuff but it is not just off the ground from the bush or woods, there's dumpster snooping, yard clean ups and moving house garbage. For this you need to go into "vulture scavenger" mode. Think it, want it, and the prize will present itself. Just have what you want in your head (it's called positive re-enforcement) and wait for manifestation, which *will* happen. Some states in

Australia and other countries have council day where you ditch unwanted things on the front yard and for a week people will cruise by and help themselves to all the goodies. After a week the council truck picks up the leftovers. This is a brilliant way to encourage recycling, there's a saying "one man's trash is another man's treasure" and I can tell you that women can be just as bad as I'm one. You will get the odd person that just puts out rubbish, I must admit this could me too, but it (rubbish) was once my treasure that I had hauled in from some dubious place and had great plans to do something special with, but never got the time. I am more discerning now.

As a partner you may go through the fe/male hoarder's stuff from the shed or cupboard without their knowledge and put it on the front lawn. However this should never be their own lawn as the scavenger fe/male will just pounce on it and haul it all back and then become Gollum-like and protect his or her precious hoard nearly as fiercely as if you ditched his/her lucky underpants. So the goodies should be placed a few doors down, or the smarter ones will put it all a block or two away, which is a much better idea as the scavenger will go snooping when they walk the dog or "just out for a walk" both of which they only do at certain times of the year, and which just happens to be on the same date as "put out" week! And guess what? They don't even recognize the fact that their own stuff is missing but they haul it home and say, "Hey look what I found," and yes it all comes back again and into the shed to be admired and coveted till the next time you ditch it. Consequently, take it further away and they might come home with something you can actually make use of.

The best thing about free hunter-gathering is being out in the bush or forest, the beach or riverbank, or hills and dales. Farms also have an abundance of really cool stuff from rocks to bones to general discarded treasures. So get into real hunter-gatherer mode and as we say "bum up, nose down," go sniffing for the treasure that's on the ground.

A nice hunter-gatherer day out is to take some food and drink and relax and take it easy, perhaps have a picnic alone or with friends whether it is the human or the four-legged variety. The four legs are good at bone and stick gathering but also may be much more protective of their find. They cannot be reasoned with, so you have to be quick if they find something interesting, because they will become obsessed very quickly with their archeological find. They will however probably negotiate if you have something to trade, the sort of beasty version of coffee and cake. You cannot take something without giving something back, whatever form it may be. Even if Rover doesn't hand it over, it's nice having a one-on-one with your furry friends in the great outdoors. They get to experience the hunter-gatherer instinct that is usually dormant at home as they can't pee on the legs of the table, chew on your shoes or try and dig a hole through the carpet. Have a go at doing it their way, get out and get dirty, scratch in the ground and watch the looks you will get from furry friend, first it's '"What the — !" followed by "You idiot you have no idea I will show you how it's done." Doggies don't need to talk as we do. They have the most wonderful facial expressions. So while Rover is showing off and already dug halfway through to the center of the earth, you can try grabbing the goodies that are being excavated by the not so observant hound digging away. Because you are now the victor the coffee and cake rule comes in and you have to share food and drink with furry vanquished and enjoy each other as you relax and watch nature do its thing all around you. It is a truly a grounding experience. I warn you again, do not gloat that you have the treasure that Rover actually found. If furry friend does not give you a good nip on the bum in retaliation of your smugness, the goodies will be sniffed out at home, even after you spent weeks, sanding, polishing, and generally beautifying it and will be re-claimed and chewed on. This I know from experience.

What I like too, is the picnic with friends as you all get to relax and be with each other sharing the trees, the earthen ground, the voices of the birds and the rustling of the beasties that are curious, a lizard wandering by, the ants that are slowly encroaching on the picnic basket (Yogi Bear in miniature), spiders on their silver webs, and field mice.

If you pick up twigs and other things, just make sure there's no one home. Do check out what you are picking up, digging up, turning over, especially at certain times of the year. We have some lethal beasties here in Australia and you could be disturbing or destroying their habitat. If someone did that to you what do you think you would do? So be safe and sensible and consider the environment you are checking over, this is

beasty real-estate and comes at a high price if you mess with it too much

Not for the squeamish is the **Road Kill** category! Yes, you can pick up feathers that you find floating around, or be given a mummified bat found under a tree, even several hollow cow horns dug up at a friend's farm, these are usually horrible but just need a bit of cleaning or cleansing but sometimes major scrubbing. Road kill is different, especially with recent ones and can be quite emotional but can also be funny depending on who you with. Obviously do not go with me, I will either be laughing or chopping and crying all at the same time. I think because I am in the medical field of work that I am a bit de-sensitized, but I do not like the dismemberment of an animal that met their maker and I treat them with all due respect and thank them, acknowledge their life on this earth.

So there you have it — hunter-gatherer. Go out and about and enjoy the treasures you will find.

Pamper a Pagan

One question I have constantly heard from non-pagans and even a few pagans is, "What sort of gift can I give a pagan friend?"

Well that's easy, something off the ground, something made with love, something handmade or even bought. If they are a friend you will know what path/s they follow which will help. Even as you are finding your own way in the magical realm your friends can see what pagan treasures you like and it is fun watching their faces as they sheepishly give you a pretty parcel. After you unwrap the parcel to reveal a stick of wood, you look at it lovingly and creative ideas come flooding into your head as you plan and visualize what the stick will eventually look like as it sits on your altar as a prized and beautiful wand.

You perhaps won't end up with stuff from a Catholic bazaar if people know your beliefs but then again that's where the craft part comes into it and all things can be changed to suit us. I have seen an old altar boy frock turned into a fabulous robe by some sewing of magical symbols and a bit of ribbon. Come to think of it the new religions did take a lot of pagan stuff and made it their own so it's just a case of returning it to its rightful form. Anyway here is a list ideas that you can write out to put on your fridge just to get you started and which are not in any particular order of importance.

Plants

Whether they are seeds, cuttings, potted, or even cut flowers it doesn't matter but try to suit them to the season or the sabbat that is nearest to the occasion in question. For instance at spring (Ostara), some bright multi-colored flowers and greenery would be suitable, while at Yule a vase full of holly or mistletoe.

In general it is an idea to choose herbs, flowers, trees or shrubs in pots, that can be planted in your garden, that way the plant can be enjoyed straight away as the receiver can get down and dirty then sit back and watch them grow over a nice glass of wine or ice cold beer that came with the gift. The good thing about this is that you can sit next to the friend and enjoy it both together as you sip, yak and pick dirt out of nails while smelling like manure, and flicking off dirt. Now that's a great idea for a bonding session! What bliss sharing some plant watching time, and the best thing about it is every time you go over to visit the friend you have a plant that you check out its progress.

Candles

You can't go wrong with candles, big, little, fat and thin, different colors, smells, short, long. Do try to go for natural wax though such as soy, or natural beeswax (the honeycomb type). You can also buy or make candleholders of all descriptions from clay to glass and from fancy chandelier types to something quirky.

You can make something yourself out of modeling clay which you don't need to fire. Alternatively drill a hole in a small log, or throw some sticks together, glue or tie them up then put a candle or two in the middle and *voila* you have a rustic candle-holder that is original and looks really great. Remember to make it look like a bunch of kindling. Don't forget to place the candle in a glass or some other protective vessel or it will burn down and become real kindling and you will be tossed on top by the arson squad after your friend has rearranged your bone structure.

Books

Think about this one first and make sure they don't have the book you have in mind. I'd go for a gift token especially for new books. If like me you prowl the secondhand bookshops you can find some fabulous treasures, the older the better. You can choose books on gardening, plants, farmers almanacs, herbs, flowers, moon cycles, zodiac, or look up some pagan authors and go in armed with a list of names and see what's there, particularly the old ones as they are hard to get hold of as they are out of print.

Subscriptions

Why not get a year's subscription to the magazine your friend likes or pay for their membership to the organization they are in or would like to be in. In Australia the three main magazines that I know of would be *Spellcraft* and there's *Spirit Guide* (this one is more New Age though). There is PANinc (Pagan Awareness Network) and they have a magazine called *The Small Tapestry*. Your local pagan Federation usually has a magazine subscription, and don't forget Ireland's own *Brigid's Fire* magazine. Most pagan magazines come out quarterly.

DIY magazines and books

DIY books or those on natural cleaning methods, and gardening without poison, or natural beauty treatments are a good choice as a gift.

One of my favorites is actually *Woman's Weekly Home Hints*, it's old but has some good material in it as it was written before the shopping isles were filled with thirty-two different kinds of product that ultimately do the same thing. There are magazines and books on natural products from cleaning to making your own cosmetics, as well as looking after the beasties in your household. The good thing about this is that you can give the book or even a print out from something on the internet perhaps on natural cleaning methods, buy the ingredients and shove the lot in a basket and make it look pretty. Plan a day that you and a friend can meet to actually make the product together. (Take note: The friend usually leaves when the booze is gone and it's time to test out the cleaning power on the moldy shower screen). Alternatively in the same way plan a day of natural beauty treatments that may be more attractive to your friend and encourage her to stay longer.

Pressed items
This is sort of time consuming but will be much appreciated. Find a big old fat book with plain paper (not glossed) and a brick or two. Do your hunter-gatherer bit to find flowers and leaves. I actually do this all year round so I have the flora from and for all the seasons. My favorite items to collect are leaves. I have oak, elm and amber leaves all pressed and beautiful showing the colors of the season in which they were harvested. I keep them in boxes with the season written on it. If you are the patient sort of person start collecting now so all your flora treasures will be dry and flat ready to be boxed for next year. While you are waiting for everything to dry keep an eye out for boxes, there are all sorts available at bargain shops. I prefer plain cardboard ones as these can then be decorated. Be careful if you are cutting things from the neighborhood as this can lead to embarrassing situations. When you have an arm load of the neighbor's garden with scissors at the ready, you discover cranky old Mr Wimpledonk is

standing right behind you. I suggest being nice and asking permission as the Wimpledonks of this world do not appreciate their one and only prize rose disappearing in the middle of the night! Even if it wasn't you this time you will still get the blame. I think you have worked out now how I know this!

Off the ground

How easy does it get but to pick things up from the ground? Remember though it's not just any random rubbish you may come across. Make an effort and have a bit of forethought of what you looking for. Go for a picnic or even just a stroll in the woods and check out all the sticks and rocks that look interesting. When you bring them home it might be idea to clean them up a bit, sand the wood, or give the rock a scrub. If you are at all artistic, research symbols and such and give your stick as an end product such as a wand or staff. Sticks that have had a light sanding are equally appreciated.

Other items you could collect are feathers. Collect all the feathers you find and put them in a nice box. Do not ask for them as I did. I have several boxes packed with feathers of all descriptions. I spent three months picking up feathers till I had to ask them to stop. I am amazed any of the birds in my area can fly, they must all be bald. Skyclad birds just don't have the aerodynamics that makes them graceful, so next time you see a naked bird say thank you because some idiot witch in your area wanted feathers.

This next suggestion will appall some of you but is also something to think about. One of my friends (who is a non-pagan), gave me a mummified bat that she found in her back yard. This bat now resides in a clear plastic sarcophagus (ex-chocolate box) laying on red satin and looks awesome, a bit like snow white in her glass coffin waiting for prince charming to kiss her awake. I have had no takers on kissing my bat so she will remain reposed and honored in her box on top of the DVD's.

If you are brave you can collect bits of road kill, a wing, claw, tail but be prepared to treat it by drying it correctly (barfing your guts up yet?) there is nothing worse than giving a gift that is decomposing even as you wrap it in pretty paper and don't forget to thank the spirit for their gift.

While hunter-gathering we often come across rubbish skips (large metal bins) and some of the stuff that goes in there with a little imagination is really good for transformation. Once you have permission and dive in and have a root around.

Garage sales are another option. Visit them late, most of the time the owner will be happy to dump on you everything that is left for next to nothing. This could be a win or lose situation as you could end up with the odd treasure and a lot of rubbish to get rid of or you could end up with just a lot of rubbish. Be cautious and have a bit of an idea of what you are looking for and think outside the box (have a read of the hunter-gatherer section too) as you'll be amazed at what you can transform into a lovely gift.

Pouches and bags

This involves sewing or looking for some plain bags and decorating them. Simple bags are easy to make either with a machine or hand sewn. Go to a fabric shop and check out the scrap bin. I made some bags to keep my crystals in out of scrap suede that cost next to nothing. While I was watching TV I churned out several bags that were strong and durable enough to carry my crystals. A friend made me a shoulder bag that is compact but still I can still fit much in and I use it at every pagan event I attend. I did add a bit of bling and jingly bits to person-alize it, but it has been most useful.

Shells, rocks and driftwood

Along the beach or even river bank is a minefield of treasure. Go for a pleasant stroll and check out the great free stuff that has either been washed up or is just lying around a riverbank. Make sure there are no creatures home or you could get a nasty bite when you disturb them. Hermit crabs are particularly nasty and have the bite power of a bull mastiff.

Jars and bottles

Search through secondhand places, or recycling centers and you will find there is always an interesting array of glassware. If they are without lids you can buy corks at hardware shops. You could invest in beautiful handmade bottles which will cost a bit but are worth having for the sake of beauty alone, however if you want to use recycled items when you run out of vegemite, jam or some such food item, soak the jar/bottle and remove the labels and paint the lids. These will be great for storing dried herbs, resins, eye of newt or dried bats. The list is endless

Terramundi pots

These Etruscan pots have been around for centuries in fact for nigh on 2000 years. The modern versions are still made the same as their predecessors. The round pots have a slit in the top but the rest of the jar is sealed and they are about the size of a smallish soccer ball. When you buy one (available on internet shop sites), on a piece of paper write down a wish and pop it in the pot. Whenever you have small change or even paper money that is spare, feed it to the pot. You cannot get it out without smashing the pot and they are so lovely it's a good deterrent not to smash it. When the pot is full and you have no choice but to smash it you will be surprised at how much is in there. Of course putting in higher denominations and paper money will mean an even nicer surprise.

Crystals

If you don't know about crystals, ask at the shop or look it up on the internet or in a book. You could also choose anything that takes your fancy. Crystals have a way of coming and going in our lives, so when you are buying crystals for someone have them in mind and the crystal will show itself.

There are all sorts of ways crystals are presented from rough to polished or carved and it really doesn't matter which you choose. Be guided by your instinct and you will choose the right one. If in real doubt, buy a birthstone crystal that matches the person in question.

Dried herbs

These can be bought at shops in packets and jars but as you do not know what process they have been through if possible pick fresh ones and dry them yourself (see herb workshop). I have several methods of drying such as cut and hang them to dry in a warm cupboard or pressing them. My usual way is to put them into a bamboo steaming basket. I lay them out separately in between layers of paper towel. I then put the bamboo steamer basket over a dish that contains chunks of Himalayan crystal rock. This dries quickly and effectively depending on the herb and whether it's woody or soft. Remember there are some herbs that can't be dried easily but you can instead make into oil or paste, or freeze. Buy a good herb book.

Oils and essences

You can make your own but this can prove difficult, but they are freely available to buy. When buying, read up on what the uses of the oil beforehand. You may be lucky enough to have an alchemy store nearby that can make up something special up for you.

Another simple gift is to go to a natural beauty store and pick up some homemade soap or other beauty product. Check the item is indeed all natural with no animal testing.

Incense

The range of incense is endless and comes in several forms, the most popular are sticks, cones or loose. At most rituals it's preferable to make your own incense. The alchemy store can also make it up for you. Don't forget when giving as a gift to put in some charcoal discs to burn it on and if the person doesn't have it, a flameproof container. There are a variety of containers you can use and once again these can also be utilized from junk you find on your travels. If you are making a dish for burning incense make sure the base is heavier. You can add sand or rock salt under the disc too as they still get quite hot.

General

If you are reasonably well off you can pay for your friend to attend a gathering they want to go to. Alternatively, go to their favorite shop and get them something pagan related and hopefully you will know them well enough to know their style and what they like. You could take your friend with you so they can pick out what they want.

Other and cheaper ways to give a friend a gift is to provide a service in offering to babysit their animals or kids so the parents are free to go to a workshop or event. If you are on a kid friendly event with them offer to look after the little rascals when their parents want to go to a workshop, ritual or talk, and that way they won't be distracted by bored kiddies.

Giving gifts to pagan people is pretty much the same as giving a gift to anyone else (though I doubt any non-pagan would really go for a stuffed bat or a jar of newt's eye balls), all you have to do is put a bit of thought into it.

If all else fails you can rely on the bottle of alcohol such as mead, some interesting teas or the old favorite of taking them down to the pub for a celebration feast.

8

Harmonia's Guide to Pathways, Deity, Divination, Nature, and Herbal Lore

Finding the Right Pathway

When I started off on my present pathway I was distracted for three years, before finding my way back.

I had started with simple ways. I loved to walk in nature, in fact preferred to walk anywhere. I dabbled in a little folk magic for many years and had varying interests. Later after having fully turned pagan I had settled into a routine of growing herbs, nature, divination, folklore (always an interest) and Otherworldy journeying all of which was very much my idea of being a witch. I was someone connected with the old ways. My aspirations were towards the cunning woman who worked with herbal remedies, folk magic and healing. In addition, my favorite divination methods were scrying with my mirror and crystal ball, and most of all, my runes. My other interests were meditation and visualization, and I had astral traveled since a small child. I occasionally had waking visions, and saw spirits and strange mist patches along with auras and energy.

One day I was walking past a book shop when I spotted a book on magical practices and another on Wicca. Soon after, my interest in Alexandrian Wicca and a higher form of magic became an obsession. I spent three years studying. I had been more interested in Culpeper than Agrippa who now gripped me along with Paracelsus. Hermeticism, secret societies, and a number of other things soon followed. In short, I was carried away.

I soon found the long rituals tedious and being solitary was not the easiest route to being an Alexandrian witch. Then one late summer's day, I was walking the dogs at twilight. It was a beautiful evening and I could hear the birds singing their evening chorus and it was strangely peaceful and still. The sun had already disappeared below the horizon and neither night nor day I walked on enjoying supernatural nature all around me. Soon ahead of me I saw two rows of willow trees on either side of the path. This wasn't unusual in that area, but what was strange was the energy that I could see darting between them and a strange mistiness around them. Hardly daring to, I walked through the middle becoming an essential part of the flowing force. It came as a sudden realization, I had ventured away from my original pathway but this was where I belonged, in (or within) magical, supernatural, unfathomable, yet beautiful, nature. This was the turning point in my spiritual journey.

Later I contemplated what I was doing. I thought back to what my idea of a witch had been and how far I now was from that. I went straight home and rid my altar of unnecessary items including the books with formal rituals. I evolved into a Hedge Witch which suited my natural abilities and interests. I am not sorry I drifted and believe this was a necessary straying to ensure I knew what I wanted without doubt.

It can take years to find a comfortable place to be in, something that fits you, the correct spiritual pathway. It is a journey which can be longer than mine or shorter, difficult or easy, hazy or clear. Good luck with yours.

Deity

Deity is different for all. Some pagans have one deity; some have dual aspects of deity, the female and male, and some pagans have multiple deities. Some pagans may have one or two chief deities but will call on others gods or goddesses. Others will have one universal deity which encompasses a number of minor deities and so it goes on.

It can take some time to build up your own connection with

deity or even to discover what deity means to you. For many people deity is connected with their interests which could be Celtic, the Northern Traditions, Greek, Egyptian or Mother Earth or Nature. Some might take their deity from different pantheons.

I will start with how I perceive deity. The chief deity for me is the Earth Mother to whom I have put two faces for ritual purposes. She is Brigid in the spring and the Cailleach who rules the winter months. I use two other faces, those of Aine and Danu specifically in the summer and autumn.

I connect with my deity every time I step out of the door. She is the earth beneath my feet, the land, the plants and trees, and everything you see in nature. But there is a dual aspect for although the sun is part of the whole of Nature, he is male, but then the moon is female, the oceans and rivers are also female and the wind is male. The creatures of the earth are male and female too and the spirits of nature, so there is a both a female and male aspect of Nature for me. I call though on the Mother for help in times of need. She is the whole which binds us together, for we are each a small part of the whole. I feel her presence as something real. I do not picture her as a definite being but more as a presence. If I try to imagine Mother, her image is a huge white figure that flies through the air, with wide arms who gathers us all in under her wings, so we are all one in her care. I sit humbly in the landscape as much a part of the landscape as are the insects, birds, animals, grass, trees, flowers, wind, rain and clouds. We are all one, all connected — as above so below.

Connecting with Deity

To further my own connection with deity, I often walk in the lanes, fields and forest, around my rural home. I feel or breathe in the essence of my deity as I look at the landscape.

Deity for you may be something completely different. You might have a connection with Brigid (various spellings), and to further that connection you could visit the sacred wells, of which there are many dedicated to her in Ireland. Or if your deity is Aphrodite you might consider a visit to Cyprus where she emerged from the sea and has a temple. The Northern pantheon might appeal to you and many pagans do visit Scandinavia to connect with their gods and goddesses.

If you are not in the position to do this for financial reasons or because you live far away in the US or Australia, then you might connect with deity by evoking or invoking them in ritual.

You might also talk to your deity, have images around that connect or remind you of your god, goddess, or pantheon. Reading as much about your deity as possible within a mythological context will also help. Immerse yourself in the culture of your deity, be it Celtic, Greek, Northern, Egypt, India or indeed Nature.

Tips

- Talk to your deity on a daily basis.
- Connect with your deity in a monthly ritual or magical or spiritual working.
- Evoke or invoke your deity when you feel ready during a ritual.
- If appropriate read about your deity within a mythological context.
- If appropriate, learn about the history of your deity.
- If your deity is the Earth Mother then go out and be with her and connect with her in her own setting.

Meet Nature

Becoming familiar with and comfortable in nature is spiritually relaxing, physically calming and healing. Reading this may help you determine if you have an inherent feeling for nature.

Do you see driving along narrow country roads as a bore? When you are out walking from one place or another, do you pass by trees and plants and not give them another thought? Or do trees talk to you, the winding brook chatter, the birds sing to you and the wind whisper?

I am lucky to live in a remote farmhouse in rural Ireland. Perhaps you do not live in or near rural areas but are drawn to them for vacations, short breaks or days out. Perhaps it is a garden or park you are attached to, or you have a yearning to dig in the earth and grow things — your own herbs for instance. Your dream might be that witch who lives on the edge of the village, surrounded by countryside, with herbs tied to the rafters of your cottage, and you dabbling in your kitchen and concocting brews (a bit like me). Possibly it is nature spirits and faeries that draw you. Or you love to dance in a downpour feeling the soft rain on your face or run barefoot through a meadow. Children often do this as they have uninhibited natures. For us we often have to lose those inhibitions of looking foolish that we have gained through our lives. Even if you don't think you have these inherent feelings, then reading this will hopefully help you to become a nature loving person.

Being at one with nature, may appear a cliché, but in fact has much meaning. Every living thing in this world is part of this world. We are all one, part of each other. Nature is important as is our environment.

"But I live in the city," you may say. Even the city has elements of nature, the sky, the rain, the wind, the grass in the park, and the birds, insects, trees and flowers in your garden, or the house fern in your plant pot. Nature is everywhere.

I see energy. I have had this ability for ten years. I can see it coming from everything, people, on myself, trees, in the air, traveling between gateposts, from cups and vases, everything. Everything is made up of energy. Everything is connected — one. The trees do talk to me, the winding brook chatters, the birds sing to me, and the wind does indeed whisper to me. This is called interaction. These things do interact with you if you take the time out to make a connection with nature.

For instance, a line of mature birch trees close to where I used to live, were chopped down as the ground was no longer supporting them well enough. It was awful for me watching them disappear day by day when only a few days before I had been watching the first signs of the leaves opening and the promise of spring. Then they were all gone and I collected two wands from the debris. One day about a month later, the leaves of the willows in the same lane were all out in leaf and walking past them I heard a tree whispering loudly to me. I looked up and saw the fresh new green of the birch leaves rustling in the breeze, and rejoiced that one tree remained hidden among the willows. Further away from the other birches it had been missed or left. I paid homage to the tree, put my hands on it and wished it a long life. The tree had informed me that it still existed for me to enjoy its beauty.

When you walk past a fenced-off meadow, even if you are tempted, you generally don't climb over that fence to walk in the meadow if it is owned by someone else. Yet you are free to enjoy looking at the beauty of that piece of land. It is strange to think that someone *owns* that piece of nature. Can anyone really own it? Can anyone own nature? See the land as being purely borrowed to graze the animals or grow a sustainable crop. In future when you walk past fields and meadows see them as a small part of the larger whole. The land is not owned any more than you are because you are married or belong to an institution or organization or have an employer, you are also borrowed. You are a small part of nature just as the meadow is and belong to a larger whole. You are as free as nature. When visiting other countries see the landscape as part of the whole of nature rather than belonging to that one particular country. See yourself as a part of the whole of nature and it will make all the difference to the way you not just view, but *see* things.

Being aware of events of nature, to listen, smell, touch as well as see, will help you connect with nature. Nature is not just what you directly see in the countryside or park, it is part of us and we are part of it.

Part of loving nature and gaining a connection with nature as a pagan, is to experience it. Nature is mutable — wild, serene, terrifying, beautiful, devastating, magnificent, uncontrollable, joyful, destructive, and life giving. Loving nature is accepting the wild along with the serene, the destructive along with the life giving aspects of it.

Pagans carefully watch the seasons change and celebrate it with festivities, from the first signs of rebirth in the spring to the ripeness of summer, to the collecting in of the sustainable harvest, and the resting period of the dark winter months. We follow the waxing and waning of the moon and tides. If you live with the cycles, are part of them, and don't wish for the end of one season and reject the start of the other often with negativity, but accept each one and flow with them, then you will become more in tune with nature herself. By wishing away the seasons, you are wishing away your life. Live the seasons, live your life to the full.

Nature Spirits

Nature spirits can be elemental spirits such as gnomes and sylphs or faeries such as elves and dwarfs. You might meet them on a hedgeriding or shamanic journey. There are plenty of faery sightings still particularly in Ireland and on the Isle of Man (UK) and other places such as Cornwall also in the UK. My uncle saw two faery men when he was ten years old and living on the Isle of Man.

To see faeries, look out for them in your peripheral vision, they are there. Even if you never see a faery, you can still communicate with them. Go outside and speak with them directly remembering you tend to get what you deserve rather than what you want. Never ask for too much and ensure it is to do with gain that it is through your own efforts, such as a new job, or more work. Always thank them but not overly so as some faeries don't take kindly to being thanked. Leave a gift out such as cream, butter, or a small crystal. They will only take the spirit of this in most cases. Remember just to go out sometimes and have a general chit chat. We are convinced we have a house faery in our cupboard, which keeps opening the door and make loud bangs every now and then.

Giving Something Back to Nature

Down our remote country lane among the beautiful pine is the perfect place for you to dump your litter. Old chest freezers, furniture that is past its sell by date, deer carcasses, even bags of household waste can be dumped. And you walkers who love to dress up in your walking boots and waterproofs and tramp up the lane and on the designated forest walks to brag about your healthy ways, why not throw your empty Red Bull cans and plastic bottles into the hedgerows and verges. I love to take a bag down and collect them to put into my recycling. So feel free to come our way and dump away...NOT!

We cannot avoid those who litter, so when you go out for a walk I cannot think of anything better than to collect litter especially those plastic bottles and bags that are strewn in the hedgerows, lanes and on the beach. It takes centuries for these things to degrade so why not take them home and pop them into your recycling.

I first started doing this when I was out with my dog talking to nature spirits. In the meadow my dog picked up a plastic bottle and carried it with him. Following his excellent example I picked up some litter on the way back that I had initially ignored. We both carried our litter home. I have been doing it ever since. Unfortunately, our beaches in Ireland are used by people who just leave their rubbish. Now instead of going for a romantic evening walk, my husband and I take bags and collect litter which has been left behind and put it in the bins which remain half empty.

If the opportunity arises join projects to clear woodland, streams and rivers, and other places of debris and litter. Alternatively, join in with your country's annual litter collecting day if it has one.

Visualization Exercise: Connecting With Nature

Go outside and to a place of nature, whether it is a garden, park, in the countryside or by a lake or the sea.

Now find a place to stand or sit comfortably and follow the example of the visualization below. Keep your eyes open.

I see the whitethorn tree in front of me. I mentally walk towards it. As I approach it I can see more and more detail. The leaves are a fresh green and it is covered in snow white blossoms. I can see the bark of the tree and reach out to feel its roughness. The thorns scratch at me as I reach through the branches. Touching the trunk I feel close to the tree as if I am a part of it. I begin to blend into the trunk like a dryad. My arms reach out and become branches, my body the trunk. I am strong. The wind rustles through me and I reach out to it. My fresh green leaves and pretty white blossom are like a ball gown. I am dressed to impress. Hard as it is, I retreat out of the tree and stand once more in front of it.

I now see the daffodils on the hillside. I single one out and approach it. I look at the trumpet, and touch the smooth petal. I smell the daffodil and breathe it in. Now I shrink down until I am the same size as the flower. I embrace it and become part of it. I can feel the optimism of my yellow bloom, a bee comes to drink my nectar and I give it freely. We have a relationship like husband and wife, mother and son. I rejoice. Now I peel myself from the flower and return to my normal size.

I see the lake in front of me. I approach it and watch the gentle ripples of the wind on the slate grey. A swan swims by. Wading into the water, I feel the coolness gently lapping at my legs. I go deeper and deeper until I am swimming. I feel so at one with the water that I begin to liquefy and become part of the lake. Fish swim within me and a swan floats on me. I am free to just be. I become myself again and approach the swan. I stroke her luxuriant white feathers, and her long slim neck. I move closer so I am swimming with her. Blending into her I become part of her. I preen my feathers, and spread my wide wings to shake them to resettle my feathers. Stretching my long neck up I feel pride as I glide across the lake. I leave my swan and swim back to the shore.

Continue in this way, becoming different parts of the landscape or seascape you see before you. This way you will learn that everything in nature is connected. We feel more of it — more relative to nature.

Things to Collect When Out in Nature

When you are out and about in nature there are various items you can collect for use in your practice. You may need a small book on tree identification. When you can identify a particular tree or plant it can be very satisfying.

Wands and staffs

If you go to a wooded area or forest, you will find an abundance of windfall branches of varying widths. If you source the wood from near a grove of particular trees, such as oak, you can be fairly sure from which type of tree it comes.

For a staff you will need to ensure that the wood is not too heavy for you if you wish to use it on walks, as your arm will soon be aching and it is likely to be quickly discarded. Ensure it is also the correct height or be prepared to trim it down.

You can strip off the bark if you wish and sand and varnish the wood ready to be adorned with your choice of decoration.

Alternatively, you can leave it be in its natural state. Personally, I prefer wood this way and seldom do anything further with it.

When looking for a wand you should use your instincts. A wand is made of wood that has magical properties. Popular choices are hazel, willow, apple, birch, or any magical tree or nut wood. I have wands of hazel, birch and willow.

The recommended length for a wand is from your elbow to your middle finger tip or about 45 cm (18 inches). The width should be large enough to carve your rune symbols on but not too wide that it is hard to wield. At least the width or double the width of your index finger will suffice.

You may have read that you should cut a wand from a hazel tree of not more than one-year's new growth, at dawn, on a Wednesday, and so forth. On the other hand, this is rarely possible for various reasons. This is where your instincts come in.

Try to use a windfall piece of wood, rather than take it from a living tree, and bide your time when looking for it, or let it come to you. After you have your wood, if you can identify the tree from which it came, leave an offering. Otherwise leave your gift at the tree closest to where you found it. An offering can simply be water or a crystal buried at the root.

Once you have your wood you can leave it as it is unless the bark is flaky. So don't feel obliged to add fripperies as it will only disguise the natural beauty and is unnecessary.

The bark still remains on my wand after many years and still looks the same.

You can varnish and decorate the wand if you wish. Again I prefer to leave it natural as I feel varnishing it will block or destroy some of its natural energy. Try looking at the natural beauty of the wood before deciding.

Runes and Ogham sticks

Venture out and find some windfall wood with which to make a set of runes. Runes were said to be cut from a fruit-bearing tree. This could mean any type of fruit, such as apple, pear, or walnut. Wood from any one of these would be ideal. There are other trees that bear fruit even though inedible. One of the sacred trees is a good idea, and these include oak, alder, ash, hazel, and holly. Otherwise try the wood of any sacred tree which does not bear fruit, such as the willow. Failing that, don't worry too much all trees are magical and sacred, and any suitable windfall branch will be fine.

Some trees, such as some apple trees will not have a suitable branch as often they are rather crooked and gnarled. And you might find hard wood such as oak rather difficult to cut and carve. Whichever wood you choose and even if you not even know what sort of wood it is, a good straight branch of about 30 cm or (12 inches), or one with just one or two curves (but it will need to be longer), is ideal. I would suggest finding a longer piece or more than one piece to allow for mistakes.

Going for a walk in woods or the park after a windy or stormy day, is part of the process of making your runes. If you can see the tree from whence the branch came, then thank it by pouring some water at the base. Put your hand on the tree and whisper your words of thanks or of course a tree hug is beneficial to you to and connects you to the power of the tree.

You need to let your wood dry and season before use. Watch out for wood that is so dry it easily breaks. If you wish you can smooth the surface of the back and front with sandpaper, but leave the edges with their natural look and with the bark intact if you prefer.

You can buy an electrical pyrograph (wood burning tool) from a DIY, craft or hobby shop, or from the internet. With this you burn the rune symbols onto the wood. You can do the burning or carving within a ritual or circle. Then at the same time you can stain the runes with red paint or ink, or you can leave them as they are.

You can polish, varnish, or wax them if you prefer to do this then and wait with cleansing and empowering until the next day in a second ritual. Or you can make the runes without using a ritual or Circle and only use the ritual for cleansing and empowering. Experiment first with odd pieces of wood and see what works best. There are no hard and fast rules.

A note on varnishing; the wood will get dirty and lose its color, as wood is porous. However, although my views may not correspond with those of others, I have mentioned before that I prefer to leave wood as it is.

To make runes with pebbles you can look on beaches, by rivers or on the land.

My first pebbles came from a river bank (I only collected exactly what I needed), and I used red ink to inscribe them and did not add any varnish and have had the same set for many years already without problems. They can be carved using a carving tool and then stained with red.

Red is the traditional color for staining, and it is thought that perhaps blood was used. Some thoughts are that this was symbolic of blood rather than actual blood. I wouldn't personally use the following advice occasionally given of staining with menstrual blood; it is up to the individual. However, the meaning of runes can be positive and negative. Menstrual blood is a powerful archetypal symbol but has both positive and negative aspects. We often add negative characteristics to menstruation ourselves just by calling it a nuisance, or "the curse," or just by sighing when we have a period because of the associated pain or heavier than normal flow. In the old days it was sometimes viewed as unclean. Of course we also view it as positive and we receive relief from menstrual flow, and of course it also points to fertility and the end of one cycle and the beginning of another.

Cutting yourself to achieve a good blood supply is not advisable or necessary and you could injure yourself and end up being carried off in an ambulance.

I use indelible red pen (only kept for this purpose) to mark the rune symbols on my stones. Normal ink, paint or natural dyes are other alternatives. If you find red is not suitable for the material, then I would suggest gold (associated with the sun) or perhaps silver (associated with the moon).

On your walks you can collect thick twigs of wood with which to make a set of Ogham sticks (Robert Graves version). A set can be made with one particular type of wood such as beech, but also of the types of wood of which each Ogham stick bears its name. It will take a long time to find all the woods, if not years. Ensure the wood collected is broad enough on which to carve a symbol (if this is your intent) or you will have wasted your time. Again a pyrograph can be used to burn the symbols into the wood.

Out and About at Sacred Sites

In getting to know your local pagan community, try arranging visits to sacred sites such as stone circles or dolmens. You can advertise in your local pagan press, online or ask any friends you know if they are up to it.

In the autumn I arranged to meet with friends to visit a hermitage, well and cave. Going up a steep hill to the cave was precarious and I made a mental note to wear more suitable footwear the next time, though I only fell over twice and the rest of the time hung onto a friend for dear life. The hazel wood there was magical and we all had a lovely time finishing up by visiting a crystal shop on the coast and having some homemade soup in the local café (although one of us could not resist the chocolate fudge too!).

Two of us decided with another friend to meet up again to have an early morning pathworking in the cave. Before my friend arrived to pick me up there was a storm and the wind was howling accompanied by torrential rain. It quickly cleared though and off we went.

We all had waterproof clothing and this time I wore my wellies (Wellingtons/galoshes). With two jackets and jeans I thought I would be fine. We also took a blanket and cushion to sit on and some water to drink.

It was a twenty minute walk from the road and ominous black clouds began to gather in the distance. We soon felt the first few drops of rain but made it into the cave in good time. We had a few tealights with us as the cave was rather dark.

Someone had been there before us as there were a couple of empty tealight holders already there. The visualization out in nature was particularly magical. We could hear the rain drops and the wind rustling through the hazel trees for added effect. When it was time to leave, we collected up the tealights and the ones left by others (you would be surprised at what litter we collect from sacred places). People come to visit probably brag how wonderful and special it was and then throw away their Pringle packets, empty jars and plastic drink bottles giving no thought to the land, the people who live there, the sacredness of the place or to Mother Nature herself. They are too selfish to give a thought to what damage they do to this beautiful landscape.

Anyway I digress, so back up to the cave. After we left the cave it was good to know that the wellies had a good grip and I slithered gracefully downhill. It was raining harder and harder and we had a short visit to the well, drank some of the clear water, and set off for the twenty minute walk back to the car. By now the driving rain and fierce wind was making it difficult to walk. I just kept my eyes on the ground and ignored the fact that the rain had now seeped through both my jackets. And I soon discovered how uncomfortable jeans are when they are wet! By halfway, water had somehow soaked all the way up and even my knickers were dripping wet. Back at the car while the others stripped off some of their wet clothing, I wrapped myself in the blanket I brought with me to save soaking my friends car seat. It was an uncomfortable journey back to my house where we all dried off and had a lovely warm drink. And guess what? Yes, we were exhilarated by the experience. Being outdoors in all the elements is what it is all about — getting to know and experience nature.

Places to visit
Stones circles are great to visit, especially those that are free to go into. Dolmens, ring forts, megaliths, portals and wells are clear

favorites. If you don't have such things where you live or even in your country then magical hills or mountains, along with forests, rivers and lakes. In Ireland for instance the rivers Boyne and the Shannon have legends attached to them. Any place that has sacred significance will be suitable.

Back in the 90s I went with a group of friends on a midnight jaunt to St Cybi's sacred well on the Lleyn peninsula in Wales. It took us ages to find it as the villagers were notorious for switching the road signs. We took every turn at the crossroads presuming that this was so, only to find that in fact the road sign was pointing the right way. We had to climb a wall, and walk through a church yard and field before finding the well. Sitting around in silence on the levels above the water was a humbling, spiritual, and for some, spooky experience. A truly magical place.

Weather

Most of the time, sites visited are in normal country areas, and rain or stormy weather or heat waves should not normally stop you from going on your PDO (Pagan Day Out). However, if you are going to a high or mountainous area then don't go if snow is threatened or heavy rainstorms. Do not go if you are ill or have recently been ill, unless you are fully recovered. Take plenty of fluids if it is a hot day and wear a hat. Prepare well for the unexpected weather as well as the expected, taking a survival kit if necessary and a most importantly a map. A torch might also be handy for dark places or if you are out later than you had planned. A cell phone would also be a handy item. Think what would happen if you were stranded overnight or owing to an injury and what you might need to have with you. Tell someone where you are going and what time to expect you back.

Things to do

You could plan to have a ritual at your chosen sacred site or do something as simple such as dowsing the area for energy or perhaps have a picnic. A group pathworking or guided visualization might be suitable. Read up everything you can find about the site you plan to visit so you gain a sense of the ancestral history. Perhaps one person can give a talk about the site to everyone else.

Lessons learned
- Take items for your comfort, especially blankets and warm clothing if it is cold weather.
- Take something to sit on if required (we were glad we did as the ground was rather cold and rocky).
- Take food and water. This is especially important if you are going to a remote area, as is correct clothing, and to tell someone where you are going.
- Take waterproof clothing if it is wet, warm clothing if it is cold and the right footwear for the occasion. It does not matter what you look like, only how comfortable and well prepared you are.
- Take a torch.
- Take a map.
- Take a cell phone.
- Take your litter home with you!
- Car share!
- Tell someone where you are going.

Herbal Lore
As pagans and witches many of us have an interest in herbs. We may use herbs in healing, magic and of course cooking. Please do buy a number of books on this subject to compare and contrast as they can widely differ and also if you want to work with harvesting herbs at particular moon phases or astrologically sympathetic times.

To obtain herbs we can visit a health store perhaps, or buy

online, but we can also grow our own and find wild herbs in the countryside.

Talk to your herbs when picking and using, to tell them your purpose and enhance their power.

Searching the Hedgerows and Fields for Herbs

1. I will start with rule number one about wildflowers and that is do not consume what you find without making absolutely sure you know what it is you are eating. For instance hemlock has many look-alikes and is very poisonous.
2. Rule number two is also very important and that is many species are protected and even whole areas, make sure you know before picking anything. You should find information on this on the internet. If you are picking a common herb in an unprotected area then make sure you do not take the root and only the top so it can re-grow much like the plants in your own garden.
3. Finally, be careful where you pick your herbs. Leave them if they are close to a busy road or in a popular dog walking area.

Growing Your Own Herbs

When growing your own herbs you will need a small patch in your yard/garden or a window box or similar.

When choosing a patch in your yard/garden, find a spot near to the house and close to a path. The reason for this is you may need to collect your herbs at night or during bad weather. You don't want to traipse through mud to get to it, or struggle down the length of the garden in the darkness. The traditional place for an herb patch is close to your kitchen, but this might not be possible as you may well have it paved in that area or it might not receive enough sun. If that is indeed the case then find another suitable but convenient place.

Prepare the ground with good environmentally friendly compost. Your herbs will need space so plant with plenty of room for expansion. Section off separate areas with pebbles or stones or provide separate pots for those plants which spread such as mint, peppermint and lemon balm. Use natural pest repellents if necessary, personally I don't use anything, and let nature do the rest.

The first year you may well get carried away and find that some of the herbs you hardly use. If this happens then replace them the next year with something more useful. Remember to plants flowers too, such as lavender, chamomile and roses.

Harvest the herbs when they are at their best. Hang them in bunches or lay them on trays in a warm dry area. When thoroughly dry, take off the leaves and/or flowers and put them into airtight jars of dark glass, or store in a cupboard or dark area. The light can cause your herbs to deteriorate more rapidly. Replace yearly with your fresh stock.

Some herbs such as mint and parsley are not so easy to dry and deteriorate and sometimes go brown, but you can freeze instead. You can also buy a book on herb knowledge, their uses, and how to store them, at any good book store.

My tip for choosing plants and start simply with the most well known of herbs such as parsley, sage, rosemary and thyme, mint, basil (summer months only in colder areas), bay, oregano (again summer and shelter somewhere in winter in summer areas), lavender, chamomile (from seed), roses, and lemon balm (Melissa). You can use all these in teas, remedies, cooking or in magical practices, with many having more than one use.

You can buy pots of herbs from supermarkets and although I have heard people say they are not suitable to plant out, I have found the opposite.

Herbs in Healing

Many herbs have healing abilities. For instance in my garden I have self-heal and clover. Both of these can be used for herbal remedies. Self-heal is excellent as a gargle and antiseptic, and red clover is said to improve hot flushes in the menopause and also relieve congestion and as a general immune system tonic. I am not going to go into the healing properties of herbs as everyone should check for contraindications. Herbs should be used with great care as with any medicine as they may interact with your own medications and cause problems. They may not suit you or you could be allergic to them. I would suggest going on a course of herbal medicine. Other than that, do triple check your sources to make sure that any particular herb is suitable for you. Most of all, when collecting herbs, (sorry to repeat) please be careful of identification as herbs can look alike, for instance Cow Parsley looks very much like the very poisonous Hemlock. When I was a child and went on walks with my aunts who were teenagers at the time, they used to point to what I now realize was hemlock and tell me it was called *Mother's Death* because if you touch it your mother would die. Needless to say, my sisters and I did not dare touch it.

Begin simply by making natural remedies with herbs you know best and are sure of identification and possible side-effects.

Herbs in Magic

Herbs can be used for incenses for meditations, ritual, and for magic. They can also be used as an ingredient in spells, in sachets for magic and cleansing baths and more.

Nicolas Culpeper

Dr Johnson said, "Culpeper, the man that first ranged the woods and climbed the mountains in search of medicinal and salutary herbs, undoubtedly merited the gratitude of prosperity."

Nicholas Culpeper a botanist and physician was at first an

apprentice to an apothecary and later his wrote his *Complete Herbal* in the mid 1600s. He went out into the countryside to collect his herbs and used a combination of his knowledge of herbs with astrology to treat his patients. He was highly respected. He was accused of Witchcraft in the English Civil War, but eventually died of tuberculosis at aged thirty-eight in 1654.

Although many of Culpeper's remedies still apply, we now have to take care and look to modern herbalists for accurate information as herbs have now been tried and tested for medical properties; Culpeper is however still useful for the astrological side of herbs and research. I have used his ideas for astrological properties of herbs below where they apply. Otherwise I have used one or two of the various planets associated with that herb. In assigning an element to an herb I have used either Culpeper or the "nature" or basic essence of any particular herb.

I would suggest beginning with some basic herbs as above in growing herbs. You can also purchase herbs if you cannot grow your own, pick your own, or they are protected in your area.

Looking back at my list for growing the magical properties of each herb are as follows:

Parsley

According to Culpeper, Parsley is an herb of Mercury. It is also an herb of air. In this context it is useful for communication. I add it to a selection of herbs for flying incense (see Astral Travel) and it is used in flying ointments. Parsley also repels negativity and can be one of the herbs used in a cleansing bath for purification.

Sage

According to Culpeper, Sage is an herb of Jupiter. According to sources, this herb is said to be a plant of air or earth. It is another healing herb and promotes healing of placed around someone in need of healing. It can be added to a sachet and put in the bed of the sufferer. Sage is also a cleansing herb and therefore can be used in the purification bath sachet. It has long been known to promote longevity and immortality. Use it also for psychic work and divination.

Rosemary

According to Culpeper, Rosemary is an herb of the sun and of Aries the Ram and is therefore a fire plant but some sources quote this as a plant of water. Rosemary aids memory and can be used in incense. It absorbs negativity so can also be used in the sachet of cleansing herbs for baths. As a known herb in matters of the heart, Rosemary can be used for love (see love spells in *Principles of Basic Magic* under ethics). Use sparingly.

Thyme

Culpeper tells us that Thyme is an herb of Venus. This plant is also a plant of air. Use it when courage is needed. I use this in incenses for psychic work. For restful sleep and protection against nightmares, use in a sleep pillow or sachet for under the pillow, or tie to the bedstead above the bed. Thyme is also a cleansing herb.

Mint

Culpeper tells us the spearmint is also a plant of Venus but also said to be a plant of Mercury and this also applies to mint. A plant of Air again it is useful in psychic work. It is an herb that can uplift your spirits and I have to say that mint tea certainly does. Use it in incense.

Basil

This herb is not included in Culpeper but is a useful herb for magic. This herb is an herb of water and of Mars and is commonly used in money spells and to attract prosperity. Basil is useful as an herb of protection, and the warding off of evil entities. Use also for love and faithfulness.

Bay

Culpeper tells us that Bay is a tree of the sun and of the astrological sign Leo and a fiery herb. Bay is a major herb for protection and the warding away of negative witchcraft or curses. An herb of many benefits, use for attraction of wealth, for prophecy and for pleasant dreaming.

Useful Flowers We Often Buy as Cultured

Below are some cultured flowers you also may find useful

though they also often grow wild.

Lavender

According to Culpeper, Lavender is an herb of Mercury. I would not be without lavender as it has multiple uses. An airy plant it can be used for love, as an aphrodisiac, for calming, sleep inducing, psychic work, purification and protection. Lavender has a wonderful perfume and can be used to flavor teas and added to incense not just for the above purposes but also to improve fragrance.

Chamomile

Culpeper informs us that the Egyptians dedicated this flower to the sun. Again this fiery (but also associated with water) but calming herb is good for psychic work and for pleasant dreaming. Use also for protection and purification.

Rose

Culpeper tells us that different species of rose are ruled by various planets. Red is Jupiter, White is the moon, and Damask is Venus. The rose is also a flower of air and fire. Most roses come under the astrological sign of Libra. Damask rose is a good old-fashioned rose used in healing, cooking and to make rose water. I use rose water on my face for beauty purposes every day. I dry my own rose petals (they are very expensive to buy) and use as follows: love attraction (red rose); luck (yellow rose); purification (white rose). Also use for protection, purification, and divination.

Useful Wildflowers and Herbs

What better excuse than to go out for a walk and collect some wildflowers. The list below may or may not be available in your area.

Mugwort

According to Culpeper, Mugwort is an herb of Venus and of the astrological signs of Taurus and Libra. Of Water it often grows on wasteland and near water. I used to collect mine from close to the river. The scent of the flowers is lovely even when they are dying off. One of the most magical herbs and one that I hate to be without, mugwort is a potent herb for prophecy, psychic work and to promote astral projection, hedgeriding or shamanic journeying. Mugwort is an herb of protection and can drive away evil entities. To identify it, look it up on the internet and in books on wildflowers.

Ragwort

Another wildflower I would like to include and which Culpeper says is an herb of Venus. Ragwort grows in pastures and is poisonous to cattle and other animals. You would have to consume large amounts to do you harm as would animals, but still I would not take it as a medicine. Use it for protection. It was commonly said to be used by witches to ride upon at night. I often hold a sprig when I hedge ride in a symbolic way.

Meadowsweet

Culpeper places Meadowsweet or Queen of the Meadows under the ruling of Venus. This grows prolifically in the fields and meadows. I picked mine from the field attached to my home here in Ireland. Meadowsweet sweetens incenses adding a lovely fragrance. An herb that gladdens the heart many people use it in teas. Magically and as a plant of Air it is used for happiness, love and for peacemaking.

Herbal Exercise

- Go into the countryside or even in your garden or along the roadside and seek out a flower or herb of which you don't know the name. Take photographs for identification and for future identification, or take along a wildflower identification book. Try to do this as often as possible during the spring and summer months.

* Go off to your garden centre or even supermarket and stock up on some herb plants. Replant them in a small patch in the garden, or into a window box or larger plant pots and place in a sunny position. Watch they don't dry out.

9

Out and About in the Otherworld

Outdoor Meditation & Visualization

Meditation

When you meditate, you empty your head of everyday thoughts and worries. Meditation is good for you to clear your mind and you will find it relaxing and therapeutic. Meditation can help heighten your intuition, reduce stress and induce a sense of well being. Things that may have been puzzled you prior to meditating, such as relationships, the world we live in, and who is the inner you, may become much clearer after meditation.

Choose a quiet place for meditation which has as little distraction as possible. Find a comfortable position to sit in whether this is the lotus position, sitting crossed legged, or sitting on your legs. Alternatively, if these positions are impossible, try sitting upright in a comfortable chair or in a reclining chair. Do not lie down unless you really have to, as you are likely to fall asleep.

If you are in a city situation and think the everyday noises will distract you, then wear ear plugs. I find burning incense also helps bring me into a state of relaxation.

Try breathing easily and naturally through the mouth.

Some people find it easier to empty their mind if they concentrate on a single image, such as a waterfall, candle flame, tree, or a triangle, square or circle or a piece of fruit such as an orange. Outdoors you could pick on the sound of the trees rustling or sounds of crashing waves. If you find other thoughts creeping into your mind, bring your focus back to your chosen image or sound.

You can also use a mantra to help bring your mind into a meditative state. Repeating the mantra over and over will help focus your mind and relax you.

At first, meditate for short periods perhaps ten minutes building to twenty minutes. There is no restriction on the time you should spend meditating, but a general guide is for periods of ten to twenty minutes two or three time a week. The more you practice, the better you will become. However, be wary of using meditation as a way of escaping from the real world. If you find it rather difficult to maintain concentration, try this exercise when going for a regular country walk or a walk in the park, or just when you are walking to work or school. Look around you. What do you see? Don't think about anything but what you see, hear, and smell. Don't think about troubles, problems, the past, the future. Keep yourself in the present. If your mind wanders, as it invariably will, bring it back to the present. This exercise will help your concentration when you meditate.

Visualization

First of all, what is visualization? Visualization is all to do with imagination and the creation of pictures in the mind. It has some things in common with meditation but instead of just emptying your mind, you also concentrate on an imaginative vision such as a journey into the Otherworld where you may or may not meet a wise man, power animal, or loved ones that have passed over. This is often called pathworking. Visualization is also used in spells to concentrate power and to imagine the spell working in a certain way or to evoke entities into your sacred space. To visualize, you need to be able to empty your mind of every day clutter in the same way as meditation, and concentrate on one image. This is often a door or portal through which you will pass.

The following exercise should be practiced for a few minutes a day. Find a quiet place outside preferably with sounds of nature. When you are settled close your eyes.

Visualize in your mind's eye, a door. It is made of heavy oak. Push the door open, you will find it surprisingly easy. Behind the door you can see a beautiful meadow, the sky is deep blue with a few fluffy clouds, and the sun is shining. It is very inviting so you step through the door. You leave the door open behind you and walk through the grass. Look around you. Is the grass long or short? How does it feel underfoot? What can you see, hear and smell? Maybe there are buttercups and daisies and different meadow flowers, or some Willow or Oak trees here and there. You may see butterflies, flitting from flower to flower. You may hear the trees rustling in the gentle breeze, or the bees buzzing as they collect pollen from the flowers, or the birds singing. Breathe in the scent of the fresh grass, and fragrant flowers.

After walking a short while you will come to the edge of the meadow up ahead. The landscape becomes rougher. There are boulders dotted around. You hear running water. As you make your way carefully through the rocks, the sound becomes louder; you are coming to a waterfall. It becomes very rocky, and you climb down between the rocks which feel cold and wet to the touch. You come to the bottom of the waterfall. It is powerful and the water is thundering down. You can feel the cold spray on your face. You find a big dry boulder to sit on and reflect for awhile. After a few minutes you sense that someone or something is coming. A messenger comes to you. What form do they take? They whisper something to you, or communicate it psychically. What thought suddenly came into your mind? They walk away. You get up and turn back towards the meadow. The way back seems easier now. You retrace your steps until you come to the open oak door. You step back through into your own world.

Practice this exercise regularly until you are really in this "other" world. You may also learn the answer to questions in your life, things that may have been puzzling you. If you like, you can invent your own variation on the meadow theme. Perhaps you go to the ocean or a lake, or mountains.

Many people use a form of visualization to rid themselves of negative thought or worries they have. This is done by throwing negative thoughts into a piece of water, such as a lake, river or well. See them as words if you wish. If you follow the above visualization exercise until you reach the waterfall, instead of waiting for the messenger, throw all your negative thoughts and worries into the water and watch them float away. Then return renewed and optimistic.

This can be repeated in actuality at a piece of water or in the bath tub. Stand as close to the water as is safe, and mentally throw all your troubles in watching them sink or float away. If in the bath tub, add salts, purification herbs and oils to the water and then let it drain away while still in it.

Guided visualization

I use guided visualization or pathworking for people who have had little or no experience of meditation or visualization but want to experience it, or in healing.

Guided visualization is when you take someone on the same journey you would take yourself in visualization exercises such as the one above. You need to be practiced at visualization before you attempt this with someone else. Teaching visualization to others is helpful for those who are a little afraid of what it might entail.

If the subject is ill they can lie down in a comfortable place, such as a sun bed. Make sure that you will not be disturbed and do not have anyone else with you. You can close your eyes and guide the subject on the familiar journey that you visualize. Describe everything you see and speak in soothing voice in the second person, present tense. For instance say, "You can see a heavy oak door which is beautifully carved. You find it surprisingly easy to push the door open. *Before you is a forest — ,"* and so forth.

When you reach your forest clearing you should already have something in mind that your subject should see; this might be a chosen person such as a wise man, witch or shaman who may answer questions for them. Alternatively, you can leave it open and suggest to the subject that they can see something or someone come into the clearing, what that will be is up to them Remember to pause to allow the chosen person to speak their message or for the subject to see and experience their image.

If you have decided this is an exercise of throwing negative feelings and problems into the water then give the subject time to do it. After a short time, bring your subject back through the door and gently bring them out of the visualization. A friend of mine who was terminally ill and whom I guided in visualization saw a bright golden light at the river; she told me it was "God"(as she saw God) and had great comfort from it. Visualization can be a great comfort to us all.

Animal Companions
Animal companions are those creatures who accompany us on Otherworld journeys or work with us psychically.

Familiars
In past times, familiars were deemed to be an evil spirit, usually in animal form, but also an imp or demon that the witch or other person dealing in magical practices, employed to carry out spells and bewitchment. This was particularly so in the witch persecutions and almost anything from domestic animals to birds and insects could be suspected of being one. The accusers thought the familiar to come from the devil himself. They believed the witch to change herself into her familiar so she could go about the countryside unseen, doing her evil deeds.

Many contemporary witches and pagans do indeed like to have familiars, more often cats, but sometimes dogs. Others will have toads, birds, reptiles, rabbits, or anything else really. Some people try to forge a psychic link with an animal, which then becomes a familiar. Others believe that familiars will naturally be attracted to them, and will reveal themselves through constantly wanting to join in with the magical work. Many familiars will be domestic pets that reveal themselves by insisting on joining in with magical work, or constantly coming into the circle, though some people think that a familiar should never be a pet or domestic animal.

Familiars help to empower spells by adding their psychic powers to your own. They may enhance the energy of your sacred circle or space. Familiars have superior psychic powers (as do many animals), and can warn you of impending danger, whether physical or in the form of negative energy. My son saw a spirit once in his bedroom at the old farm where he lives. The two small dogs of the house had woken him in the night demanding attention. My son sat up in his bed and stroked them trying to settle them so he could sleep. The dogs turned and began to bark just as my son saw the spirit floating across the floor. They had obviously seen it too and by this time had stood up and were barking madly. My son sees spirits but if he did not have the ability then the dogs had certainly given him fair warning that there was something lurking.

Familiars can also take the form of psychic messengers. As a psychic messenger, the familiar is an animal of visualization, or an absent animal with which you have a psychic link. If the animal is visualized rather than a real one, then you may request of it to assist you. Alternatively it could be a visualized real animal that you call upon in the same way.

One way to forge a psychic link with a wild animal is to keep eye contact with it. Imagine that you are transferring some of your spirit to it, and some of its spirit is transferred in return. Try to keep this up for as long as possible and until you feel it has worked. People often do this with each other to forge psychic links if one of them is going away for instance.

You will not be able to force an animal to be a familiar if it does not want to. The animal will look or walk away when you try to forge a psychic link. Always remember to respect your familiar. Your familiar might once in while feel off color or reluctant to attend your magical or ritual workings.

The Fetch

The Fetch, sometimes called the Fylgja, is a part of your unconscious or etheric self which is connected to us but operates separately. The Fetch generally comes in two forms, the animal fetch and the etheric fetch.

As the animalistic side of yourself, the side you often keep hidden from others, the fetch represents your character. The animal fetch will take on your own characteristics. If you are a sly person then your fetch may take on the form of the fox. Odin was always accompanied by two wolves, perhaps these were represent of his courageous nature.

As the etheric side of you, your spirit double, it is said that it only appears as a woman figure, though some say it only does so to a man. Others maintain it appears as a woman to a man, and a man to a woman. The latter is rather like Jung's anima and animus, which we must get in touch with as a part of individuation. This fetch stays with us all our lives but may attach itself to someone else on our death.

The Fetch is the part of you that appears in visions and otherworld experiences. If you can form a bond with your Fetch, you can achieve a state of perfect wholeness (as with Jung's process of individuation). The fetch is also said to both communicate with and carries messages between worlds. Once you achieve an affinity with your Fetch, you can call upon it as a psychic messenger, or to help contact spirits or to aid you in your general life and with magic.

The fetch is also said to appear as an apparition warning of impending death. It appears as the double of the person who is about to die, a sort of living ghost, doppelgänger or wraith. I have had some personal experience of this. Many years ago both I and one of my sons saw his doppelgänger. He was twelve years old at that time. We lived in a modern house built in the grounds of an old Victorian chest hospital where Tuberculosis had been treated. It was a Friday night and the children had stayed up late watching a film. I had decided to go to bed. I had my hands full of things I was taking into the bedroom. As I passed my son's bedroom (not the one who sees spirits), I clearly saw him standing in the doorway. He was wearing his school shirt and socks (no trousers). I was walking quite quickly but stopped abruptly when a few steps further on I heard his voice coming from the living room. I stepped backwards and looked into his bedroom and there was no one there. I carried on to bed, with a shiver rippling down my spine. I forgot about it until two days later the same son came running into the living room in a panic. He told me he was walking past his bedroom and had just seen a boy sitting on his bed. He was wearing a school shirt, no trousers and was putting on his socks. The creepiest thing about it, he said, was that it looked just like himself. He was clearly spooked (especially when I told him my own experience), and so was I. After much discussion we decided it was a warning. A few days later my son told me of a problem he had with his urine being dark. He had mentioned it before but I had brushed it off telling him to drink more water. But this time, the warning of seeing his double stayed with me (and the fact that the apparition had worn no trousers emphasizing the lower body), and I went to see what he was showing me. I knew straight away that what I was seeing was blood and that my son had a serious problem and so phoned the doctor. My son was admitted to the hospital the same day with a serious kidney complaint and kept in for a week (the illness being a lifelong autoimmune disease).

The fetch then can act as a warning of illness and not just to portend death.

Power or Companion Animal

Power animals (sometimes called Totems) are spirits that can accompany you, guide and protect you in the physical world, on the Astral Plane or in the Otherworld, and even in your dreams. Most people go on an Otherworld journey when they want to meet their power animal and this is the method I used to meet mine.

I often go on Otherworld journeys and one particular time had passed through my portal and deep into the forest; suddenly I could see a girl. She was about fifteen years old, and had long fair hair plaited in two pigtails hanging in front of her shoulders and with her was a large white ox. She was wearing peasant dress of long ago. An instant later I became that girl or took her place. I had my arm stretched up and over the ox. Standing as high as my shoulder I could feel the warmth of it. Its great curved horns did not frighten me, and I could see that its short coat was smooth and shone. I stood there for some time and then found myself returning from the journey back into myself.

I was amazed to say the least. The ox generally symbolizes strength and strength is most often the quality I need. I now call on Ox to guide me and we have had adventures together.

I now also have a white horse. Horses are something I have also had an affinity with over the years. I am also a horse in Chinese astrology. The rune Ehwaz (horse) means much to me and with Uruz (aurochs a wild ox) is my favorite rune. In this context the horse is a comfort to the restless. Ehwaz is a rune of good partnerships progress, movement, and mobility. I would add adventure and movement to the horse's qualities. Uruz is strength often inner strength and is a courageous spirit.

Accordingly, your power animal is one that you have often felt an attraction to. You may have always wanted to own this animal or bird, or actually do. You may have collected these animals in the form of ornaments, such as rabbits, or frogs. This animal may have frequently appeared to you in dreams. Power animals can sometimes be mythical ones like the gryphon or dragon. You can read more about this in Hedge Riding below. You can more than one power animal or animal companion guide. I also have an almost lifelong attraction to squirrels (in Norse mythology a squirrel lived in Yggdrasil the world tree in connection with mischief). For me personally, the squirrel has a connection with home and security (another meaning is that of gathering, planning, saving, and being prepared, and it does not know the meaning of defeat). I have also had a lifelong attraction to the Giraffe (to some cultures a symbol of the supernatural), and even now want to have a model or even toy version near me. I wonder when they will turn up.

Yours might be the bear, a raven, the dolphin, a goat, lion or the dove. Although you may well have more than one, you will not need them all at one time. They will come to you as needed and throughout your life you might add more, while others will drift away. Ox appeared in spirit to me rather than in solid form, the same day that Horse appeared for the first time during an Otherworld journey in a cave.

Experimenting with visualization and pathworking exercises can help you connect with your power animal or animal companion guide. Once you have mastered visualization, it will become easier to focus on calling up your power animal. You can meet your power animal on a shamanic or Otherworld journey, in Astral Projection, or in lucid dreams.

Concentrate on your power animal before sleep, and request it to come to you in dream. You can also do this in visualization. Invent a way to contact your power animal by creating a ritual in which you call upon it. Use this way every time and it will eventually become easier. Try to become your animal to you can take on its particular qualities, in difficult situations. Become the fox when you need to be crafty for example.

Dance with your animal in reality. Put on some suitable music or drums and dance around the room taking on the form of your animal.

Keep pictures or models of it close to you to help you get to know it/them, or wear a symbol of it as jewelry if you can find it.

Your power animal may have a personal meaning for you, don't dismiss this as animals can have many different meanings depending on each culture.

Buy a good encyclopedia of symbols (always handy), or a dictionary of symbolic and mythological animals. You can also find various dictionaries on a web search.

The Familiar, Fetch and Power Animal are not there purely to do your magical bidding as sort of personal magical or psychic slave, so respect them and thank them.

A power animal is a companion guide and will help you come to terms with your shortcomings and will help you to maintain balance between the positive and negative aspects of your personality or psyche. If you can connect with your power animal it will help provide you with guidance in handling the day to day stresses and strains of life, not provide you with the power to control others.

Power Animal Visualization
This exercise is to help you connect with your power animal to aid you in your general life. It is the forest exercise I used to meet my power or companion animal. It worked very well, because I went into a natural trance state.

Prepare yourself and your setting. Make sure you are comfortable. Play shamanic drumming if you are able, or alternatively some music you usually use for visualization. Wear ear plugs to exclude any noise. Protect yourself with a personal circle of blue or gold light. Have a bind rune of protection, or a sprig of rowan in your hand, or your wand to protect you. You can also hold a clear quartz crystal as your far seeing eye. If you see any negative spirits then mentally hold up your rowan, rune or wand in front of you for protection, touching away the spirit if it comes too close.

Close your eyes and see a tree with a large hollow or cave in front of you. This is your starting point and you will pass through this portal into the forest. When you feel well placed and have the picture firmly in your mind, then you can enter the portal. It may take you sometime to travel though and will possibly take the form of a tunnel. Once through the portal you will emerge in the forest which lies close to the sea. If you instinctively feel it is the rainforest you should be in, then the squirrel, deer, bear or wolf, in this exercise become the lion, tiger, giraffe or monkey.

It is dawn as you pass through the portal and venture onto the forest path. The sun is beginning to come up as the moon disappears through the trees, melting away the early mist. It is a magical time, not night and not yet day. The veil between the worlds is thin. It rained earlier and the water drips rhythmically through the branched canopy overhead, splashing on your face, refreshing you. Deep among the trees and foliage you see movement. A stag stands there. Squirrels run up and down the tree trunks as they begin their forage for nuts.

Something buzzes past your ear. It is a large bumble bee, and it settles on the petals of a wood anemone chasing away a butterfly. You hear a growl and something crashes through the trees. A wild pig runs across your path, it freezes for a moment and looks at you with fear on its face before running off into the dense undergrowth. You hesitate, touching your bind rune; you wait until the growling stops and walk on.

In the undergrowth you see three baby wolf cubs wrestling with one another. You stop to watch until mother-wolf appears and you quickly move on to show her you mean no harm. Further along the path there is a clearing and some wild ponies graze.

Continue in this way until you meet an animal that has direct contact with you. If it is your power animal it will stay by your side and travel with you.

If no creature attaches itself to you then continue along the path until you come to a brook. Follow it until you reach a cove. You can now smell and taste the saltiness of the sea. On the horizon you see the sun rising and the water of the estuary glitters. It will be a calm day. You hear a great whoosh as a heron takes off to the side of you, its powerful beating wings startling you for a moment.

Seagulls dart in and out of the gentle waves catching their breakfast and screeching to warn other birds away. You see something in the water — a dolphin or seal. Soon others join it. Sensing you, they come close to the waters edge. You sit on the sand close to the trees and wait and watch the magnificent sunrise.

Return along the same path when you are ready and back through the portal. If you use a drumming CD then it may well have a number of louder drum beats after a certain length of time to signal you to return.

You should take at least twenty minutes for this exercise. Take time to recover after it. Ponder on what you saw as it could be more significant than you realize. Don't worry if you do not meet or connect with your fetch immediately. Keep trying the exercise and eventually you will have results.

Dancing with Your Power Animal

The purpose of this exercise is to help you become constantly aware that your power animal, guide, or companion is with you. You will become more familiar with it through dance.

Ensure you have plenty of space preferably outdoors. Go barefoot. Put on some suitable music or drumming.

Begin by jogging visualizing you are with your power animal. Now let yourself go and move in whatever shapes come to you. Ride or fly with your animal depending on what it is. After some time try to take on the form of your animal. Become it and fly, crawl or run. Once you feel you have danced enough, come back into your own form and dance a little again with your animal. Finish by thanking him or her for being with you.

Astral Projection or Travel

First, I will talk about my own astral traveling experiences; answering the more popular questions that I am regularly asked, along the way. If you have astral traveled, then you might recognize some of the events or happenings that I have experienced.

Since I was a young child of between five and seven years old, I have had the ability to leave my body. I used to regularly find myself standing at the top of the stairs, and would wonder if I could "fly" down. Even at that young age, I knew I was not in my body, and would not hurt myself. Still, it took a long while to pluck up the courage to launch myself off the stairs and float very happily down to the bottom. It was a wonderful feeling, and after that, I did it regularly happily flying around the house.

At about twelve years of age, I was speaking to some friends and started a sentence with "you know when you go flying at night..." my friends all looked at me strangely as if I had grown two heads, so I immediately shut up. I had presumed that this was something that everyone did. After that, I kept my experiences to myself.

As the years went by, I found that I could actually launch myself from my bed and fly to the stairs, and around the house. Strangely enough, it never crossed my mind that I could leave the house until I was about forty years old after a witch friend suggested it. She recommended that the next time I was traveling, to leave the house and fly over the rooftops, as I would enjoy it very much.

A few days later, I did exactly that and a few other things too. The first problem I encountered (and a question I am frequently asked) was how to get outside. I knew that I could not open the front door, but logically worked out that I must be able to pass through it. I just launched myself through the door rather like the first time I "flew" down the stairs and the feeling of being outside was euphoric. With no limits, I zoomed straight up at immense speed and into the sky, and had a familiar buzz, that many travelers experience. At this point, I was moving very fast and went above the clouds. Up above me I could see blue but realized that I was heading out of the atmosphere. At this point, I started worrying about being able to get back. I traveled back down to the just above the rooftops seeing everything on the ground getting nearer and bigger. I could see the rooftops were shiny and wet. I saw a red car pull up into a parking space, and a young couple got out and crossed the grass in front of the houses (I did not know any of my neighbors, as I had just moved into the house). As they walked, they were discussing painting and decorating. I darted around them rather amused that they could not see me. After they went in, I decided to return to my body. Confident by now, I went through the bedroom window, and saw myself nicely tucked up and dropped back in. And yes, the red car was there the next day, and it had rained in the night. Since then I have traveled "out of doors" at every opportunity and apart from a couple of occasions, I am usually in my own familiar territory.

The first time I traveled on the astral plane during a projection experience (I have traveled on other planes during hedge riding) was a few years ago, and was the most amazing experience I have ever had traveling. I was in my bed and I saw what I could only describe as a spirit, hovering above me. It was ethereal; a flowing elongated shape, tailing off, rather like you would expect a sylph to look. I would liken it to a girl-child figure. She took me by the hand out of my body and almost immediately I found myself traveling in a world of glorious green nature. We flew together over beautiful trees, rivers, hills and fields. All the colors of nature were more vivid than in my own world. It was the most beautiful place, and I had a wonderful feeling of calm and peace. A thought came to me that this must be the place you go when you first die, and I felt there was a journey ahead. I knew that I was not to go on that journey at this time but others would. At this point, my spirit guide left me. Confident, I traveled around by myself and to explore this amazing place, then thinking I might be outstaying my welcome, and feeling privileged at having seen it, I decided to go back to my body. Here I will answer another frequently asked question; how did I find my way back? Having researched Astral Travel, I knew that I could think of my feet and that would take me back, but in fact just thinking this thought took me back.

Later among other things, I wondered if my spirit guide was my sister who had died as a baby. A few days later my beloved uncle died. I was glad that my uncle was going to such a wonderful place.

Most people when they first "travel" start out in the physical world. This does feel safer until you gain confidence, and can be fun! Because we are operating at a higher frequency during travel, we have the ability to walk through walls, travel at fast speeds, and have a more pronounced power of thought. The feeling of flying can only be described as "euphoric" and once tried you can become an addict to this wonderful feeling.

Accordingly, I have been astral traveling for close on fifty years. I have spoken to many others who astral project naturally. Only once have I come across anyone who has taught themselves to do this. That person, a witch, I spoke to about fifteen years ago had psychic abilities. Most of the people I spoke to said other members of their family also had the ability to astral project. Hardly anyone passed into the Otherworld and most travelers stayed in their own environment. This does not mean you cannot teach yourself to travel only that it is difficult and you may not succeed. If you have certain natural abilities then it is more likely, and these include lucid dreaming, being able to control dreams, sleep paralysis, being a light sleeper, and having the ability to clearly remember your dreams. Other skills might include the practice of shamanism.

Many travelers talk about a silver cord or umbilical that they see connecting to their spiritual and their earthly body. Not everyone sees this cord, which does not mean that it is not there. Some people say that if the cord snaps while traveling that you will die, as you cannot get back to your body. I personally would not worry about this, as fears will prevent your enjoyment in traveling. I would like to know where this information came from. Who came back from the dead to inform everyone that the cord broke when they were traveling causing them to die? You will not die until it is your time. Use your common sense when you read comments like this.

When I am hedgeriding (Otherworldly travel), then I protect myself before engaging in this. However, with AP (astral projection) it is not always possible. If AP happens spontaneously (and many of those who travel do not plan to do so and do not know from one day to the next, or even one month to the next when this is going to happen as the conditions need to be favorable), then prior protection is not possible. In addition, in an AP experience the traveler might not actually travel onto astral planes but stay on the earthly plane, and this is the most frequent AP natural experience for most people. However, if you are attempting to induce AP and in doing so to attempt travel on the astral planes, then there will be ample time to protect from unseen forces, and it is prudent to do so. Teach yourself to AP successes must be rare. Just as it is difficult if not impossible to teach yourself to suddenly become a clairvoyant medium (as opposed to improving psychic abilities which can be done) it is also difficult to teach yourself to astral project.

We all have abilities, just different ones. I can astral project and have good intuition, see auras and energy and occasionally spirits, have contact with spirit through vision but this is not something I can control. However, I cannot contact spirits at will, I am not clairvoyant, and I am not a gifted healer as such.

If you have spent years attempting to astral project without success why not try to seek out a new skill (the clues are often there to what this could be) or choose an existing skill you can improve upon.

There are people who are close to astral projecting as they have clues to this. They often feel as if they are about to leave their bodies but cannot quite achieve it through fear or something such as sleep paralysis which they cannot control. Some people have strange AP experiences such as spinning around on the floor, being thrown around, or barely lifting themselves off the bed or couch before snapping back into their bodies. If you do want to attempt to astral project and think you can achieve this as you are always on the fringe of it, then there are some tips below. Some of it is recapping for easy reference.

How can you Astral Project if you cannot do it naturally?

I am a natural astral traveler, but over the years I have taught myself to induce traveling too. You need to be aware of what you are doing. It is not something to be played around with. AP is always easier if you are already a lucid dreamer. A lucid dreamer is someone who is asleep but aware of it and is able to control their dreams. If you are not a lucid dreamer, you should follow the tips given here during daytime hours, so that you are less likely to fall into a deep sleep.

Lie down in a darkened room. Before relaxing be sure you are not too sleepy, so an early night is best. Concentrate on staying conscious or lucid in your sleep. Think hard about astral traveling, dismissing all other thoughts from your mind. Hopefully, you will go into a just below consciousness state (but are mentally aware). This may take more than a few attempts, and you might never succeed.

During AP you will be mentally aware, without confusion. Concentrate hard on lifting yourself out of your body. Again, you may have to try this many times, but concentration and forethought are essential.

If you should succeed then keep to your home and normal environment at first, and get used to this until you become more experienced. This environment will look exactly normal. If you come out of the AP and find that although it looked normal to you in the AP, you actually realize now that it differed, then you were likely lucid dreaming. In occasional cases it could be that you go straight onto the Astral Plane, which has happened to some people. The Astral Plane is another world that may or may not look familiar, depending on the level of it. You may meet others while "flying" there, or spiritual beings which inhabit the planes. Again it is different to a lucid dream as you cannot promote events to happen.

How do you know you are not dreaming?

When you are lucid dreaming, you can conjure up a situation or person. If you want to kiss Brad Pitt for instance, this would probably be your only opportunity to do so! In the astral world, whether in familiar surroundings or not, you cannot do this. So try it and then you will know for sure.

How do you get onto the Astral Plane?

Again it is concentration if you have not automatically traveled there or been taken. Think yourself to the Astral Plane. This is not as easy as you might think, and you might not ever achieve it.

I have heard you can meet deities and relatives that have passed on while traveling on the Astral Plane.

Sometimes you just come across them. On my second traveling experience to the Otherworld, I was traveling in a darkened tunnel which appeared vast. I continually moved forward. I could not see anything. I could however feel other people traveling, hundreds, perhaps thousands in both directions. I tried to concentrate on seeing but to no avail. There was a general buzz of excitement and murmurings that I picked up telepathically.

What is the difference between an OBE (out of body experience) and NDE (near death experience)?

There is no real difference. They are both out of body experiences. An OBE is astral traveling, and can be both natural and induced. An NDE experience is a natural occurrence that happens when someone is near death or whose heart stopped for a time, such as after a heart attack, an accident, or during an operation. The person floats above their body and can see themselves below. They then travel down a tunnel towards a bright light and eventually come into a beautiful land or garden where they see loved ones that have passed on. At this point, they are sent back, as it is "not their time" otherwise we would not get to hear of these experiences. Generally, people who have had this experience go through life changes, and no longer fear death.

During lucid sleep, I am paralyzed and cannot leave my body. How can I change this?

It could be fear of the unknown that causes this paralysis, but it is usually a natural thing and many people suffer this. Try not to be afraid and wait as it could be the first stage in separation. Focus on relaxing and tell yourself that it is a natural event. You may then separate after a short while.

Remember that it is you who is in control. Some people cannot gain control and spin or seem to be dragged around. Again, it is control and relaxation. Concentrate on gaining control. You are capable of stopping this. I have met one or two people who had this problem and again it was practice and patience that helped them gain control.

What am I likely to feel or hear?

Some people hear a buzzing, roaring, or high-pitched noise on separation. Others feel a vibration. I have heard the buzzing. It feels as if it is going through my head rather than in my ears.

What if someone disturbs me?

If you are disturbed when you are astral traveling, your spirit will immediately return to your body with a thud.

Will others be able to see me?

Generally, people in their earthly bodies will not be able to see you. Other astral travelers may see you, and you may see them. However, there are always exceptions. You may have heard about people appearing to relatives warning them of own their impending death. Then sometimes people see spirits, this could also be an astral traveler, no one really knows (and these are my own thoughts). After all, spirits travel on the astral plane too.

I believe there are seven astral planes. Can I travel to all of them?

Some people maintain that there are seven with each having more than one level. Each of these planes has a different frequency, and many people have reported traveling beyond the lowest astral plane, usually to the middle planes. Each astral plane becomes more spiritual and is inhabited by higher spiritual beings.

There are varying opinions on this with many other people saying that there are only three realms or planes, one above our world, one below, and one parallel with it. It's the latter one that it is said most people travel to.

Astral traveling is a quite comprehensive and sometimes contradictory subject as each experience can be very different.

Hedge Rider

Hedge witchery for me in general is experiential and a slow and natural progression of interests and events experienced from childhood and persisting all through my life. As Aristotle said, "For the things we have to learn before we can do them, we learn by doing them." Learning by experiencing is about trusting your instincts and connecting with your inner spirit.

Part of being a hedge witch is engaging in a form of Otherworldly travel called hedge riding. Other aspects of hedge witch practice include a deep connection with nature and perhaps an interest in herb lore, wildflowers, spellcraft, divination, and other general "country witch who lives on the margin" pursuits.

As a hedge rider, I can only relate my own experiences of how hedge witches practice and others may work differently. As a spiritual seeker, I am still very much on a journey and believe that it will be many more years before I can count myself experienced in hedge riding, especially as it is a solitary practice.

In past times, the witch was said to travel straddling the hedge with one foot in this world and the other in the Otherworld. The hedge is a symbolic boundary between the two worlds. In actuality, the hedge separated the witch in her cottage from the rest of the village or community. The hedge is also a form of protection keeping out unwanted spiritual visitors. For me, my hedge of protection is always that of the whitethorn (hawthorn).

The Otherworld I visit is a realm or plane which exists parallel with our own earthly reality, or is slightly above it and is a place of wondrous nature. I do not venture into higher realms. The amount of worlds, realms and alternative realities that exist differs from culture to culture and person to person. I firmly believe from my own experiences that there is more than one level. Many spirits and entities exist in these alternative realities and it is possible to meet and contact them.

It should not be supposed that hedge witchery has to be a totally solitary and lonely existence. Although the hedge witch is a solitary practitioner by nature he or she might well meet regularly with other hedge witches and pagans in general to share or discuss their practice and spiritual path.

A hedge witch will cross the hedge to seek help from the

spirits and elementals that reside there for healing, strength, spiritual enlightenment, protection, sometimes simply to look for messages or solutions to problems, and for some to help in spell work, but mostly to gain wisdom. For what is knowledge without wisdom? I would never cross the hedge for magical empowerment or for material gain for I believe you receive what you need, not what you want. Journeying can be for yourself or others. Hedge riding is an individual experience and riders work with their own spirit guides and without an authoritative overseer. Each individual seeks to grasp the meaning of their own experiences, but can ask advice of others, perhaps a shaman.

The hedge riding aspect of hedge witchery is perhaps the most difficult part of the pathway. This article focuses on that aspect alone and further study, research and practice are essential.

What it entails
Straddling the hedge with one foot in either world is not the easiest thing to do. Straddling the hedge may have already invoked some strange or even humorous images of severe discomfort. However, although your body is in this world, it is your spirit consciousness that is in the Otherworld.

As hedge witches, we travel to the Otherworld in an induced trance-like state or altered state of consciousness, achieved by various methods that suit us personally. The astral projection (AP) or out of body experiences (OBEs) I had experienced for most of my life and in more recent years the visions and glimpses of the Otherworld, the meeting of my power animal, and the coming to me of passed away family members and family pets while in an altered state of consciousness, progressed into hedge riding before I had even put a name to it, seven years ago.

Altered state of consciousness

An ASC (altered state of consciousness) means that your mind is working differently than when you are fully awake in this everyday reality. Your mind and spirit is in essence separate from your body. With ASC you are working just below the surface of full consciousness. This is opposed to the "unconscious" in which you are not aware what you are doing as it is hidden from you, such as with dreaming. In an ASC we are always aware of what we are doing. This state is often induced by drugs though I do not use them myself. Steering away from drugs or herbal concoctions, there are safer ways to achieve ASC and that is through meditation or visualisation with the aid of chanting, drumming or even listening to the beat of your own heart. Great concentration is required. With ASC we are lucid and able to control our movements, so we have to avoid falling into deep sleep. ASC is similar to AP in that in doing so we dissociate our minds from our physical bodies. With me the AP is more often than not a natural occurrence, though is sometimes induced, while ASC is always induced in a particular and ritualistic setting.

The place to start as a complete novice would be to practice visualisation skills and pathworking.

Protection

Many people advocate using protection for any Otherworld travel as there are both positive and negative entities on the other side of the hedge. We never know what we might meet there, though personally I have never had any negative experiences, but if I did it is comforting to know that I am protected.

One of the simplest methods of protection is the blue or golden pool of light generated from the solar plexus area and surrounding us completely like a force field in an oval or egg shape. We form this pool of light around us by visualising it emanating from the solar plexus area just below the breast bone. As it spreads through and around us covering us completely, we deepen the colour to strengthen it. Being aware of it keeps it in place. It will dissipate naturally in time if we do not mentally keep it there. We can hold an amulet of protection or wear one. I often hold a rowan twig or protective crystal loosely in my hand but I am also mentally aware of it. We can also ask our spirit guide or our accompanying power animal, if we have one, to help protect us. We can travel as an animal of the land, sea or sky. This would be an added form of protection rather than the only form, as animals are also prone to predators.

Animal companion and spirit aides

While hedge riding, it is common to have an accompanying animal guide commonly called the power animal or companion animal. The companion animal is often a bird, or creature you feel a particular affinity with, whether or not you have ascertained it is indeed your power animal, or a even what you previously thought of as being a "mythological" creature. You may have had synchronous events that feature this animal.

Your animal companion can run, walk, swim, or fly beside you. The companion is company for you so you don't feel alone. It will give you strength, confidence, and added protection. You might be able to communicate with it in some way but more often than not telepathically. You should also feel a deep connection with it, almost as if you are one. The characteristics of your animal companion transfer to you. Spirit aides come in all shapes and forms and are an added form of protection and guidance in the Otherworld. They can be any creature of the earth but can also be elemental spirits or other spirits you call upon for assistance.

Setting the scene

Scene setting is important to help you gain the correct frame of mind. Comfort is essential to aid concentration and minimise distractions. You will require peace and quiet, away from noise and people and ensure the room is warm, but not too hot, or use a blanket. Play drumming or chanting or anything that will help induce a trance-like state. If you have a CD of drumming, choose one of fifteen to twenty minutes and perhaps one with louder beats at the end to signal you to come back. With more practice this can be extended. I use one of approximately thirty minutes. Alternatively chant your favourite mantra or one you have put together yourself for the purpose. Wear ear plugs if necessary to exclude everyday sounds (turning up the volume of the drumming to compensate). Light some homemade incense that is helpful for concentration and psychic work or use a non-toxic flying ointment (both symbolic). Sit comfortably, semi-recline or lie in the dark or light a single candle. I have found a semi-reclining position best as I tend to fall asleep when lying down. I often hold a quartz crystal, symbolic of seeing beyond the beyond, a natural wood wand, and a small branch of rowan or another plant I might have collected from the garden or neighbouring countryside. If you prepare the scene an hour or so before, you will ensure you have everything you need; there is nothing worse than distractions.

Putting it all together

If you wish to attempt hedge riding and you don't need to be a hedge witch to do this, set the scene and make yourself comfortable and protect yourself. When you feel ready, begin with a pathworking exercise of passing over or though a gap in the hedge. Alternatively, you can pass through a gateway, door or portal, which leads to the Otherworld. This can be a cave, a hollow tree trunk, or the triad portal of trees, Oak, Ash and Whitethorn (Hawthorn). You can continue walking along a path or flying through the air, or swimming in a river. Then you let the experience take over and hopefully you will pass into another reality. It was through such an exercise as this that I first passed into the Otherworld. In this case, I was walking on a forest path.

The forest holds much magic for me, though flying is my favourite form of Otherworld travel.

Do not go with too much expectation or intent to begin with. Have a purpose before you travel. Try something simple like looking for a message. This message might be given to you by someone, you might read it, or see it in the form of a symbol. You could also look for your power animal. As you become a little more experienced you can try other things such as seeking healing, perhaps bathing in a holy well, or cleansing through water, or meet someone who will offer you advice. You might not achieve passing into the Otherworld for a long while but persevere. Even if you believe you have not put one foot over the hedge you might still have much to gain from this. You will know when you have been successful as you will have been totally immersed in this "other" world, and the experience will be as real as normal life. You will stay aware that you are of this world, even though your mind is in the other.

Grounding

If you are hedgeriding on a regular basis then you will need to ground yourself. You can do this before and after rituals and pathworkings. This will rid you of excess or unwanted energies. It will also help you reconnect with your own world. We can often get caught up in otherworldly traveling, and it is good to literally come back down to earth.

A standard grounding ritual is to stand with your hands by your sides and think of your body as the trunk of a tree. Be aware of the earth beneath your feet even if it is some way down as you live in a high-rise apartment. Take some deep breaths to start.

Now starting from just above your head, concentrate on draining all negative thoughts and excess energies by imagining them moving downwards through your body relaxing as you go. When you reach the root chakra area, this is the area around the base of your spine and pelvis, imagine growing roots from this area, which will grow downwards from it and also from the tips of your fingers and soles of your feet deep into the ground. Think of it the root tendrils creeping through the soft earth past the earth worms and moles and deeper though the rock and even as far as liquid mantle to the earth's core. Let the excess energy and anything negative run down the roots as they grow deep into the ground. Feel yourself anchored solidly. After you have finished take some more deep breaths and bend down and touch the ground to give thanks.

Another way of grounding yourself weather permitting, is to take off your footwear and go outside and stand barefoot on the ground for a few minutes. Relax and be consciously aware of the ground or grass beneath your feet. Connect yourself to the earth and be consciously aware of it. Or go outside and do some gardening.

Let your hedge riding experiences gradually build and grow. Be courageous and take slow steps and you never know what you might achieve.

Divination

Divination is popular among pagans. Perhaps the most popular forms are Tarot, Runes, Ogham, Scrying and Dowsing, although others might favor angel or faery cards.

Whichever we decide to use we need to know how divination works.

When we use a form of divination as a non-psychic or with limited psychic abilities, we are calling on a hidden intuitiveness to help us to interpret the cards, runes, sticks or dowsing tools, and help us with our everyday life problems and situations.

When divine, we open unseen pathways between our conscious and unconscious self (our psyche) in predicting what lies ahead. Our own instincts and knowledge from the unconscious helps us in reading and understanding what we are divining often without us realizing. As we read the signs and symbols, thoughts pop into our minds even though we might not be aware from where these thoughts come, but our instincts tell us they are correct. Subsequently, these intuitive skills will become stronger and more successful over time. The divination tool helps develop them by continually tapping into wisdom lying deep in the unconscious mind, revealing hidden truths and acting as a messenger bring them forth into the conscious mind. Jung called this wisdom, "archetypes of the collective unconscious."

I write here about synchronicity as it is quite significant when it comes to understanding the hidden mysteries of the runes. A synchronous event is one which is more than an ordinary coincidence and cannot be explained. It is when two or more outside events coincide with a psychic event. Some of these events at times include archetypal symbols, are often numinous, and sometimes there are accompanying dreams. These events happened separately and neither causes the other.

When we divine, we often look at pictures or symbols (the outside event) and they reveal to us the underlying but hidden psychic forces. Another way of explaining this is to say in the microcosm or symbols, we open our minds to the macrocosm or omnipresent energies, we would not normally recognize. These universal energies reveal past, present, and future events. The future events are not necessarily fixed, and by divining and revealing the possibilities we can change patterns, or at least adapt ourselves to them. So, in essence we are acknowledging that mind and matter are harmonizing aspects of the same reality.

So how do we recognize a synchronous event? The best way to help you understand these events is by giving examples.

I was reading an excerpt from Maggie Hyde's book *Jung and Astrology*. In it she discusses how when writing the book she was talking to others about Kingfishers and about how Jung found a dead one in his garden. No one at the dinner could recall anything about the habits of kingfishers. A few days later she received a letter from one of the people at dinner saying that the day after the dinner he and his mother had seen a kingfisher over a lake. The mother had told a story about finding a dead kingfisher five years before and had shown it to her granddaughter. The friend from dinner could not recall seeing a kingfisher before. Maggie goes on to say that talking about kingfishers around reading Jung promotes this type of incident. In this case two stories of a dead kingfisher and one live one came together in a synchronous moment.

In a synchronous moment after reading the article I went for a walk and stopped on the bridge over the River Fergus. I saw a kingfisher (the first I've seen in Ireland) fly along the fast flowing river. When it was out of sight, I turned to look over the other side of the bridge and the same kingfisher or perhaps another flew back over the bridge and right in front of my face causing me to jump back. It was so close I could feel the back draught from its wings.

I don't recall how I came across the excerpt of the book, but I was not looking for information on Jung, I had come across it accidentally. These synchronous events are such that we never forget them as they are so significant. People we tell them to also remember them and pass the story on, simply because they are meaningful. We remember events like this it because it shows us that there are forces at work that we might not fully understand. Still, we acknowledge they exist. Everything is connected as above so below.

So to sum up, if we learn to recognize and acknowledge these moments, we can explore them instead of writing them off as perhaps just a big coincidence. We then come to accept that there are things that cannot be scientifically explained, as it is impossible that they could have occurred purely by chance. The universe is not just made up of scientific facts. We don't know everything purely because we live in an enlightened age, and we can only benefit from opening our minds to the infinite possibilities. If we delve deeper into the interrelation between mind and matter, or spirit and matter, it will in turn help us in developing our relationship with our divining tools.

Appendices

Check List for Gatherings and Camps

Tent (with awning)
Sleeping bag
Sheets and pillows
Water can or bottles
Camping Stove
Gas bottle

Cauldron and charcoal
Picnic plates/cups/cutlery
Folding chairs and table
Pots and pans
Torch
Blanket or fleece
Washing-up bowl
Dish cloths and scourer
Washing-up liquid
Toilet paper

Aluminum foil
Portable ashtray

Celebration clothing
Waterproof clothing
Warm or cool clothing
Waterproof footwear
Sandals and/or jogging shoes
Nightwear geared to the
weather
Pairs of socks
Bag for immediate essentials
Medication
Toiletries
Antiseptic spray
Antihistamine spray and cream
Book to read
Paper and pen (for workshops)
Candles
Food if necessary or extra
snacks
Drinks
Bag for litter

Pagan Talk with Kimi

I am blessed to have friends from all different paths, ages, backgrounds, experience and locations from around Australia. So to finish off I asked them to answer some questions just so you can see the differences but also the similarities of each of these very individual people. I actually didn't even realize what a colorful and interesting array of friends I have. All the questions are the same, these are real people that walk our streets in day to day life have careers, jobs or school, and families, just like everyone else, so the answers should be relevant to all countries. Eight people have been randomly selected by an outside source to cover age experience and so forth these are Jonno McCutcheon, Mark, Tina Lea, Terri, Toni M. Larson, Eilan, Cam and Anna Prati (Morganna). I wish I could put everyone in here as they are all so interesting and diverse. I hope by reading their answers you will get to know the sort of the people you will meet when you are out and about in the community. Tread your journey well and enjoy the discovery of the people you are going to meet.

1. When did you first become aware of, realize, or discover the path you are now treading and what path do you follow?

   Mark: *The path you are now treading is one that should be constantly changing and evolving. The moment we have security in our environment we are no longer expanding and growing. I would say the path that I am on is one of self awareness and self development.*

   Tina: *I always was aware of a spiritual need from about seven years of age, but mainstream religions left me constantly dissatisfied and disillusioned. I knew I was different, but constantly hid it, even from myself. The death of my two year old son was the beginning of my living in my own truth. My path is my* *own and I have adopted sacred women rites from many cultures and woven them into my own life. I work with the energies of nature and the universe, but also honor, respect and serve the deities and spirits who guide me. I presently am enjoying working with African root magic and deities.*

Eilan: *I was very blessed to have been born into an intuitive and spiritual family. My father is a devout Balinese Hindu man and my mother is keenly intuitive and is of colorful Celtic descent. We have quite a few notable ancestors, including the famous Sister Elizabeth Kenny (my great-great aunt on my mother's side) and my Balinese grandmother, who was known in her village for her gifts of healing and divination. I was invested with these spiritual gifts by virtue of my heredity and my own path unfolded before me.*

It was at the age of twelve when I first became conscious of my Witchcraft and I began to identify as Pagan. It wasn't such a stretch, considering my background. The path I walk now is a highly syncretistic one involving British Traditional Witchcraft, Stregheria, Hellenismos, WildWood, Faeriecraft and my ancestral traditions of Bali and Eire. I also helped to co-found the WildWood Tradition of Witchcraft — the Mother Coven was dedicated and initiated at Samhain (April 30th) 2006. I became an initiated priest of the WildWood at Samhain 2007.

Anna: *In the late eighties I began looking for a path and read a couple of books on witchcraft, then was lucky enough to find a wonderful teacher and the rest, as they say is history. I'd call my path eclectic Wicca, for want of a better name.*

2. Are you open about your choice to family, others, work and what reactions did you get?
   Jonno: *Yes, we are lucky here in Australia. Thanks to the work of great organizations like PAN, the younger generations rarely face discriminations. Paganism is now a discourse that most people are familiar with these days. I must stress that for me,*

being a Pagan has never been a choice, it's the way I am, how my brain is wired I guess! If not... why not? If so...why? "Pagan" is not a dirty word anymore; at least not to anyone I've met! My mother said, "That's nice...can you dry the dishes?" which basically sums up my families attitude towards my religion. Occasionally they laugh at how kooky I am, but they don't ever try to change who I am. My friends are all aware because it's a bit hard to hide when my house is littered with altars, bones and stones — that said; maybe thirty percent of my friends are Pagan too.

Mark: *If you are truly on the path of your spiritual destiny then you have to be not only honest with yourself but honest with others. If you are hiding your true nature then you are destined to live in fear.*

Terri: *Yes — everyone knows. Reactions were pretty good. My family is not religious at all so there wasn't the whole "going to hell" thing to worry about. I work in a very diverse department within my company. My boss is full on Christian, another co-worker studied for years to become a Buddhist monk, and the others are either agnostic or lapsed Christians. Even with my boss there aren't any issues — we're friendly outside of work.*

Toni: *I judge if people are capable of coping with the information. My eldest son was okay and then behaved strangely. He said I could talk to him about anything but not my pathway or anything to do with paganism. Second son, didn't care one way or the other or the younger children. My partner doesn't say anything one way or the other.*

3. How did you find your first gathering? Did you go with others or alone? How did you find out about it?

   Tina: *My friend invited me to into her circle and I attended a "Woman's Sweat" after my son died. At the "sweat," we worked with a circle to create sacred space, and then we drummed and danced with fire, all together. It felt like the most* *natural way to be and I felt really at one with the other women there, who were of all ages and cultures. It was my first real taste of powerful Goddess Energy. Finally my yearning began to be satisfied and the path that I now follow opened up clearly.*

Toni: *The organizers made no effort — knowing from my registration that I was new and wouldn't know anyone. A woman I knew from Canberra — made no effort just said hello once and moved on to her friends. There were two people who saw that I was on my own all the time and made an effort.*

Eilan: *My first gathering, depending on how you define the term, was the PSG in January of 2007. However I had been to three Pagan Pride Days (2002, 2003 and 2004) in Brisbane prior to this. I found out about PSG through Witchcraft (when it was still being published) and Spellcraft magazines. I attended the gathering with my friend and fellow priest of the WildWood, Ana James. We were completely embraced at this gathering and were encouraged to hold our cone of power ritual which we repeated at the end of the gathering as it was called for again. The gathering numbered somewhere between 60-90 people and was held in a pristine valley in the Sunshine Coast hinterlands. I joined the Church of All Worlds at this event and I since been an active member of the CAW.*

Anna: *I think it was Pagan '89 and Remo and I went together just for the day. I'd read a review of the previous year's event in Witchcraft magazine and it sounded so good I was determined to catch the next one. It was amazing being among so many pagans — a whole different mind-set. I think we stayed for the ritual, but had to leave while the music (a live band) was just cranking up and it was really hard to tear myself away. The next year we went for the whole weekend with most of the people from a coven we had joined in the interim.*

4. Have you any suggestions for new discoverers (newbies)?
Jonno: *There is a lot of crap out there so make sure to keep it*

simple. One of the primary goals of the witch is to seek attunement with the land and her cycles. Be observant and familiarize yourself with your surroundings because you will find much more about the workings of Spirit out there than in a book.

Mark: *Don't turn up with an ENG Camera.*

Tina: *You need to dedicate yourself to learn, discover, taste and see. It takes time and lots of patience. Lots of reading. Lots of practice. I feel my spirituality is my own responsibility, so just like anything, what I put in is what I'll get out of it.*

Cam: *There is NO right way or wrong way. Don't let so called "experts" tell you that you have to follow "their" way of ritual or worship. To truly connect with the Goddess and the God, follow your heart, connect with the elements, open yourself up and feel the energies flowing through you. Even in a group or coven environment, everyone's connection with the Goddess and the elements is different, special and unique. That's what it's all about, "your" connection, "your" spirituality.*

5. Do you have a magical name (for want of a different word) and how did you come by it?

Eilan: *My Craft name is Eilan (pronounced i-lin) meaning "island," and it was given to me by my late Balinese grandmother around the time of the winter solstice in 2006. Before that time I went by my ancestral Irish name of Dobhair (pronounced as "door") meaning water. Everyone who knows me knows that my Craft name is Eilan as I often sign off e-mails, letters, etc. with this name. I also have a name which is shared only with the inner court of my coven and a few others, and a name that is only known by the Gods. However, when I first began to consciously engage with my Craft no name was forthcoming and I honestly didn't feel the need to own one. My given names are quite magickal, and I still believe this to be so. The names that I now possess were all given to me by my* *ancestors, my Gods and my guides. I honor them and their wisdom by owning them and using them. Beautifully, all of my names weave together well and speak with the same essence.*

Terri: *I gained my craft name during my initiation as it was part of it. My HP and HPS know it.*

Cam: *Mine is "Berggarten," it's German for Mountain Garden, my favorite variety of common sage.*

Anna: *I have a magical name that reminds me of qualities I want to develop (Morgana's magical abilities), as well as incorporating an area my Welsh ancestors came from (Glamorganshire) and including my birth name. Most people know it.*

6. Seasons are very different on this island of extremes. How do you see the changing seasons in your area and which area is it?

Jonno: *The European agrarian wheel of the year does not suit my land at all. Summer in Canberra is not a time of abundance and posterity; it's a time of heat and bush fires! Yule is not the coldest sabbat here, Imbolc is, just as the bread festival is hotter than the summer solstice, so I reject the European system because it is useless down here. I read the flowering cycles of native plants to get a feel of what's happening. Our dry patch of Earth is ever fertile — even in winter so get out there and sew some seeds, and then you'll understand the wheel of the year. We are lucky. Australia is an ancient continent with deep wisdom. Our plants and animals have much to teach us so again, get your head out of the books and talk to your land.*

Terri: *I live in Sydney, NSW. The tree outside my office window loses its leaves and the bite in the air coming into autumn and winter. The new baby magpies during spring — I love watching them grow up and then come back the following year with their babies.*

Eilan: *I live in Brisbane, in South-East Queensland. The* *climate here is sub-tropical so the four seasons of the European temperate zones are not necessarily applicable here. However, the eight sabbats are not fanciful festivals that have been created and superimposed over this land. They are definite points within a cosmic and terrestrial cycle, and thus our continued celebration of them in this country is not without merit. For instance, the four equinoxes and solstices are astronomical events. The four cross-quarter festivals (the Celtic fire festivals) are simply the points in between the solar sabbats. In my tradition we honor the seasons as they manifest in our area, but also as symbols of the mythos of our divinities. The stories they tell as the Wheel turns speak to the deepest part of the human soul, and the human soul is a mirror to/of the greater world. Even though there isn't snow at midwinter where I live, it is still cold, the days are definitely shorter, and we rug up and stay inside. We experience the same sensations, just on a lesser scale. Our DNA recalls our ancestral experiences and we are tied together through time. In my experience, celebrating the sabbats, helps to align the self with Nature, with the Cosmos and with the Community of Souls.*

Cryptozoology and Curious Creatures
by Kimi

What is cryptozoology? Cryptozoology is basically the evidence of creatures whose existence is uncertain, a science of researching for proof of animals that are considered extinct or those that are not of this world.

It is not only the misty moors of Britain, the green forests of Europe, the woodlands of North America, or the secrets of the Amazon, that have mythical creatures. Australia too has its share of mythical creatures and I was surprised how many I found when researching this subject. Though many would say they are *not* mythical as someone's *brother's-friend's-cousin* saw it (you know the same sort of person who can never be tracked down, the same person who spreads urban myths that we all know and love and which we then spread around ourselves in turn), some will say that they themselves have actually seen these creatures.

Apart from the aboriginal tribes who have an extensive array of mythical stories that tend to be kept within that tribe and culture as a whole, there is very little written in books as the stories are orally passed down from generation to generation as with the ancient bards.

I looked up Australian cryptozoology and attacked the internet with abandon, as well as books and indigenous dreamtime stories, I found some interesting information. Here in Australia we have some really ancient and diverse creatures both mythical and real. I think this is because we are considered a continent or island unto ourselves and the general animal migration over the centuries is not the same as the rest of the world.

Another source of information that I had to endure, spend money on, and suffer the odd hangover, was found at pubs in various locations. What I found out from the old-timers down at the pub was fascinating at well worth the odd headache. The pub of course is the old-fashioned internet filled with interesting people and information. In Australia this is called the *bush telegraph* and a place for telling yarns — stories sworn to be true, and also many a fib but which makes you wonder.

Everyone had heard the saying, "there's no smoke without fire." There is so much unexplained stuff out there I would not discount everything heard from some beer fuddled old codger who's farm is in the middle of nowhere and away from civilization as such, and a good place for mythical beasties to roam without the prying eyes of too many humans.

The Australian countryside is very diverse, with desert, rain forest, sand dunes, scrub, rolling misty hills, breathtaking cliffs and rock formations, immense impenetrable forest and bush land, snowy mountains and miles and miles of some of the best beaches in the world. As a matter of fact we pretty much have a bit of everything from across the globe. If you came for a visit, I would be able to dump you somewhere and you would be certain you were in your own country.

This country can not only be magnificent, breathtakingly beautiful and in contrast cruel and harsh, but also mysterious and dangerous, particularly to those who are silly enough to wander off track. People are often swallowed up by the countryside, or maybe some unseen beasty, never to be seen or heard of again. There are still vast areas that are impenetrable to explorers so who knows what is lurking there.

Australia is a large island, for example Great Britain fits easily into one of our smallest states with comfort and with room to move. Imagine a wilderness that is supposedly uninhabited but is the size of England and throw in a few areas as big as Ireland and an inland desert equal to the Sahara. These areas are so huge that it is feasible that they are inhabited by yet to be discovered species. Even creatures thought of as extinct could well be roaming the bush and mountains and only come out to see what is going on and to give some poor soul a fright and a bloody good story to tell, or of course eat them and the poor soul then goes in to the *never to be seen again* box.

Only recently the bones of a prehistoric and fantabulous creature were dug up in the desert and every now and then a new species is found. On a fairly regular basis there are stories on the news as well as down at the pub, about sightings of the so called extinct Tasmanian Tiger (Thylazine) or the panther that roams the around the blue mountains. And don't forget the Yowie, Bunyip, or Dropbear. We have some of the most unique creatures in the world such as the platypus.

I have really enjoyed researching our few but interesting mythical creatures. But are they mythical? Or are they just hiding from us the invaders of their territory? Maybe they are just camera shy.

Mythical Beasties of Australia
Bunyip (devil or spirit)

Sightings of the Bunyip are reported across the continent. The Bunyip is a terrifying creature that has been talked about by the Aborigines for thousands of years but has also been mentioned by the settlers when they arrived and the description of it widely varies. Common descriptions are that it has a large doglike head, razor sharp canine teeth, dark course hair, the tail of a horse, and flippers (though it can walk on land); it also has tusks similar to that of the walrus. Some descriptions mention horns. According to legend the Bunyip is said to lurk in and around isolated water holes, billabongs and swamps. During early settlement the notion that it was an actual unknown animal was commonly thought. There have been recorded incidences of seeing or even hearing the Bunyip, and it is said the spine tingling howl is like that of an unearthly dog or wolf.

In 1821 some rather large (horse-size) and interesting bones were found in a lake in mid New South Wales. The skeleton was named Diprotodon and nicely fits the Bunyip description. Though it appeared to be a grazing animal, it didn't seem to have a problem preying on anything that went too close to the water's edge. These elusive creatures are also said to be prehistoric survivors.

Yowie (Hominid, similar as the Yeti and Bigfoot)

The Yowie has been sighted across Australia and prefers to live in the mountains, thick bush land and forests. Reports of Yowie-type creatures have been common in Aboriginal history and continued from the settlers. Like its cousins the Yeti and Bigfoot overseas, blurry photographs have been taken as well as a plaster cast of its footprints.

Said to be a very shy creature, it stays close to its habitat so as to avoid contact with humans. There has never been a report of an attack on humans that I could find, but I do think it is fairly intelligent as it seems to have avoided full on contact with us and can escape at speed and disappear into the bush. Another report I found was that several people that were close enough to get the blurry photo say that they smelt a really fowl smell rather like wet dog or old rotting carpet with a bit of something else that was decomposing thrown in. So obviously if you are in bush and get whiff of something nasty you might be in Yowie territory. Have your camera at the ready and set it on blurry, then hope for the best.

Hawksbury Serpent (perhaps cousin to "Nessie" the Loch Ness Monster)

This one I hadn't heard about, but in my travels I overheard a conversation at a pub in New South Wales that started with "I was out in the tinny (small aluminum boat with oars) and was trying to unhook the line that was snagged. A log that was a few meters away, moved and then a whopping great head came out from the water and looked me straight in the eye then sank under the water." I asked what it looked like and the reply came back," a slimy skinned dinosaur or snake thing." As the water was murky the teller of the tale could not see what sort of feet or flippers the animal had, but other reports have stated that the creature resembled a large seal like creature but with a longer neck and that it looked prehistoric. So whatever this young man had apparently seen he rowed very quickly back to his house, changed his underwear (for obvious reasons he was scared) and then reported it to a ranger. There have been several sightings of this sea creature over the past few years, could it be an escaped animal from a circus that has since evolved to suit its habitat or a perhaps even a surviving dinosaur.

Thylazine (Tasmanian Tiger)

This Tiger looks like a very large dog, and is of considerable length. The so-called *first and only one* in captivity was about thirty kilos and measured about two meters from nose to tail, about one meter tall, probably even taller, longer and bigger. It was said to be brownish in color with short coarse fur and darker strips going down its back. These animals were basically hunted to near extinction by the early settlers, but in 1933 they were given protected status but it was too late and in 1936 the one remaining Tiger at a zoo in Tasmania died and they were classed as extinct. Even though the Tiger resembles a dog it is classed as a marsupial as they had a pouch in which they carried their young. These creatures have on an occasional basis been sighted in heavy bush land across the continent, the last known report that I could find was 1990 by a park ranger.

Black Panther

These cats are regularly reported especially around the mountain areas of New South Wales but have also been spotted in other states and different habitats such as in the desert areas in amongst large rocks formations. The most prevalent sightings and photos of the Panther are located in and around the Blue Mountains. The main theory of how the cat came to be was it had escaped a circus or that it was someone's pet who had freed it. Speculation is that it bred with feral cats as some sightings of the Panther record it as brown in color. According to general belief, the cats have remained uncaught as their habitat is in and around very dense bush that covers a huge area. The animals are elusive but several farmers have discovered chewed sheep in their paddocks. Owing to the amount of sightings, the Government is investigating as they believe it is not just an urban myth and they have concerns for the safety of small children

Megalania Prisca (Dragon of the Outback)

Thousands of years ago the forebears of the creatures we know today such as koalas and kangaroos were very different. Large, most being carnivorous and quite vicious, they are referred to as Megafauna. At one time there were monster lizards that dwarfed the Komodo Dragon which is about the size of a lion. The Megalania is thought to be extinct and was perhaps around twelve meters in length, weighing approximately 900 kilo's with its body is the size of a cow.

Though reportedly extinct, is it in fact? There have been many reported sightings in the last century up to present day and some sightings even suggest it also inhabits parts of remote Papua New Guinea. Plaster casts have been taken from soft ground after the rains and show massive lizard feet. Most of the sightings are similar in description, for example people out in some remote areas have seen what they thought was a fallen tree which then moved and ran off, this is normal lizard behavior as it basks in the sun but will scarper when disturbed.

Kraken (Giant Squid)(Mesonychoteuthis Hamilton)

This sea creature has been described by fishermen and sailors in stories and tales for centuries throughout the world. Once thought be absolute myth in the present age scientists are questioning this. One theory is that owing to global warming, creatures that inhabited the deep oceans or the Arctic areas are now being exposed, and over the years quite a few sightings from deep sea fishermen have been reported. The similarities of the descriptions cannot be overlooked, and it was only recently that a giant squid was found dead in Australian waters which measured about fifteen meters in length from tip to tip. Could this be our very own Kraken? Actually in 1925 two squid tentacles found in a whale that measured thirteen meters in length were also found in Australian Antarctic waters. Two other specimens were found in 2003 and 2007 and the remains were sent to New Zealand for study

Drop Bear (distant cousin to the Koala)

Reported sightings and attacks are from all areas of Australia, and unexplained deaths or disappearances are attributed to the Drop Bear. While they have never been photographed or captured either dead or alive, DNA from victims show they are an evolutionary step behind koalas, Tasmanian devils and quolls. Those that have survived a Drop Bear attack describe it as similar to a koala but larger with coarse fur and long razor sharp claws. Instead of cute rounded ears they have large pointy ears that can rotate like a cat. Their teeth are sharp with canine incisors several inches and a long pointy snout. The Drop Bear's eyes are reported as evil-looking with a yellow hue to them. These creatures are very elusive and very quick. They live in trees and when their unsuspecting prey walks beneath them they drop on the victim and rip and bite till they are senseless. At this point the bear drags them undercover to feed at their leisure. These bears like most nocturnal animals don't like light. Some victims that have survived used their camera flash to temporarily blind it and to give them time to escape.

Jacky Lanterns (glowing Light)

In remote areas of Australia there have been sightings of strange bright glowing orbs of light that seem to float just above the ground and parallels the surface contours as it travels. Believed to be a barn owl, the starlight is reflected in its eyes. Another theory is that it is an undiscovered bird or a relative of the dragonfly family (as they can hover) and they create their own electricity or light, much like the very deep ocean fishes.

B O O K S

O is a symbol of the world, of oneness and unity. In different cultures it also means the "eye," symbolizing knowledge and insight. We aim to publish books that are accessible, constructive and that challenge accepted opinion, both that of academia and the "moral majority."

Our books are available in all good English language bookstores worldwide. If you don't see the book on the shelves ask the bookstore to order it for you, quoting the ISBN number and title. Alternatively you can order online (all major online retail sites carry our titles) or contact the distributor in the relevant country, listed on the copyright page.

See our website www.o-books.net for a full list of over 500 titles, growing by 100 a year.

And tune in to myspiritradio.com for our book review radio show, hosted by June-Elleni Laine, where you can listen to the authors discussing their books.

MySpiritRadio